KARMIC ASTROLOGY

THE MOON'S NODES AND REINCARNATION

Volume I
In A Series By

MARTIN SCHULMAN

SAMUEL WEISER, INC.

York Beach, Maine

. . . To a New Astrology—Viewing man through the window of his Soul.

. . . To those very special souls whose tireless dedication made this book possible. To Robert J. Siegel who gave me my first glimpses; Lorraine Johannesson, whose silent efforts cleared the path; and Laura Schwerdtfeger, whose unshakeable faith moved every mountain.
To all my students whose unquenchable thirst continues to serve as a ceaseless inspiration.

First published in 1975 by
Samuel Weiser, Inc.
Box 612
York Beach, Maine 03910

99 98 97 96 95 94 93
25 24 23 22 21 20 19

Library of Congress Catalog Card Number: 83-104490

ISBN 0-87728-288-9
MG

Printed in the United States of America

The paper used in this publication meets the minimum requirements of the American National Standard for Permanence of Paper for Printed Library Materials Z39.48-1984.

TABLE OF CONTENTS

CHAPTER ONE

REINCARNATION AND KARMA

PART ONE—WHAT WE KNOW ABOUT REINCARNATION

The mystique of reincarnation has been for centuries a subject of fascination to the curious mind. From almost the beginning of time man has entertained the possibility that life is one continuous thread, with the process of birth and death only phases moving from one stage of existence into another. All life is change and all change is life, but life eternal is what the ancient masters promised and within this realm of eternal life everything changes yet nothing changes.

What is the reality of man's existence? Is it his physical life, his deeds, the principles he stands for, or is there something yet more subtle that creates and re-creates human life?

Our senses can easily deceive us, for at this very moment you believe that the page you are reading is real. But the truth of reality exists throughout the eternal mansions of time and space. There was a time when this page was not and there will be a time in the future when it will cease to exist. You can measure the page with a ruler and find that it is not smaller nor larger than a number which man has invented. Yet neither time nor space can show the full truth of the page.

It was creative thought that gave birth to the page in terms of focusing energy for its physical existence. Thought will create many more pages and when every page ceases to exist, the thought of pages will create still more.

A beautiful architectural design is only as real as the thought that created it, for at one point in time and space the symbolic structure will cease to exist, yet the thought that creates architecture will continue for eternity. The seer Nostradamus wrote many physical pages most of which are now burned or lost. Yet the thoughts of those pages are very much alive. Such is the substance of eternal life.

The thought of you is the real you; not the you as seen by relatives, friends and neighbors. The real you is not your physical body for it could never accept that its effects end at the boundaries of skin.

Time was not when you did not exist and time will never come when you will cease to exist. But parts of of you will change for during your eternal life you are going through an everlasting transformation as your soul journeys upward toward perfection.

We can see such changes in the simple beauty of a nature story. Two caterpillars were friends and spent much of their time together. One day one of the caterpillars died, whereupon his true and loyal friend began a quiet grief-stricken vigil near the body of his departed loved one. After many days of sadness the caterpillar looked up to find a butterfly staring at him.

"Why do you cry?" asked the butterfly.

"Because I have lost my friend," replied the caterpillar.

Then in all his splendor and beauty the butterfly proudly answered,

"But I am your friend."

To the caterpillar reincarnation was difficult to understand, but to the butterfly it was a fact for he transcended one physical form into another, never losing the true essence of himself in the process.

In ancient Egypt the bodies of departed souls

were entombed with their most cherished possessions
so that they might be comfortable along their future
journey. In India for many years bodies were cremated
so that the soul could rise on the ashes up to Brahma.
More recently, Indian bodies are left as food for the
birds with the full and complete understanding that
the physical shell itself is only the temple that houses
the soul. They seem to know that the same thought
that created such a temple would create new temples
as a soul needs them.

The American Indian knew much about eternal
life. The battle between the Sioux and General Custer's
troops at Little Big Horn indicates that life after death
is not only a possibility but a fact. The celebrated
Sioux medicine man, Sitting Bull, was known to pos-
sess unusual powers. He practiced astral projection
regularly, as well as displaying all the other talents
that one would ascribe to a medium.

At the time of the battle of Little Big Horn, Sitting
Bull was actually a great distance away "making
medicine," but it was his accurate prophecy of the
details of the battle that earned him his highest honors.
In the years that followed Sitting Bull discussed the
Custer incident only with his tribal war chiefs. From
them we have the most fascinating recollections of how
this great Indian mystic went in darkness to the site
of the battlefield so that he could make medicine beside
the fallen body of Custer. It was then that the spirit
of the departed general manifested to him and for a
short time words were exchanged.

Custer warned Sitting Bull that a treacherous act
by a white man against him would take place within
fifteen years. He would have no foreknowledge of it
and no medicine that he could make would prevent it.
This would be an opening of a play yet to be acted.

"The white man would cover the earth and neither
you nor I nor the Great Spirit Himself can stop the
infiltration and bloodshed that will follow. We are but
one act in the play and we have done as we were told.
In less than fifteen years we will both be on the same

side. The white man sees only white and the day will come when he will try to extinguish all men who are not white from the face of the earth. Know in your heart that I speak truth, for you and I were once brothers and will be brothers again. Be relieved of your burden, for man is an angry wolf stalking and tracking down his prey from the beginning of time to the ends of all time but you and I are more than men as men know men. Go now and be with your people. They need you more now than before. I will be with you many times when you light your pipe at night and I will be with you in your final hour as you are here with me now."*

When the conversation had ended Sitting Bull covered the face of the dead General with the silk handkerchief that Custer had once presented to him.

During his remaining years Sitting Bull remembered his night with General Custer and on several occasions spoke about it with close tribesmen. Fourteen years and seven months later this amazing prophecy was fulfilled as Sitting Bull was assassinated by government agents at Standing Rock.

Three days after he was slain while peacefully sleeping in his cabin, a group of Sioux Indians returning from a social gathering saw him appear in the hills, in much the same manner as the reappearance of Jesus.

This amazing incident can be folklore no more than the millions of pages written throughout the world of similar such incidents. Appearances in spirit form have been reported since the beginning of time throughout every nation and indiscriminately in all parts of the globe. Man hears voices, receives messages, sees spirit forms and in some instances even experiences contact with his former lives.

---

*As this page was being written, the entire room became filled with the spirit of Sitting Bull. For over an hour I was pulled into trance while he telepathed to me these exact words spoken to him a century ago.

The skeptic would discount much of this as the product of an unbalanced mind, but on too many occasions the proof of other life forms is so substantial that even the most critical mind must stop and wonder. Particularly in the instances where medical and scientific explanations fail, the process of eternal life can be seen not only as plausible, but in fact as the only logical explanation.

We know that babies are born with definite personalities which they exhibit as early as their first days in the hospital nursery. Very often these personalities are quite distinct, displaying unique characteristics, unexplainably contrary to their traceable heredity.

In India there have been cases on record of children capable of speaking foreign dialects other than those which their own familes have taught them.

In one case a young Indian girl started screaming to her mother, "You're not my mother." This persisted for some time until the family decided to seek professional help. A team of doctors, psychologists and parapsychologists was brought in to determine the causes for the child's seemingly irrational behavior. Upon much questioning the girl explained that these were not her parents, and the house in which they were living was not her house. She insisted that she lived in a yellow house on a hill in another town, and that in her bedroom in that house a cache of money was hidden under a floor board. She described the house perfectly and upon taking everybody there led them to the upstairs bedroom where raising the floor board, she took out the cache of money. Before going to the house she had even described the curtains, home fixtures and the man who was living there.

In the duration of time the house was painted, but it had been yellow in the past just as she had claimed. The man who resided there had lost his wife. It became an established fact that this girl was the reincarnation of his deceased spouse, when both the girl and her former-life husband recognized each other. Ulti-

mately there was no question in the minds of the doctors, psychologists and parapsychologists that this
young nine year old girl had been telling the truth.
Their soul love must have been so great that she felt
drawn back to this former circumstance.

From time to time we see cases of extreme natural
inborn talent. As a youngster, Mozart gave his first
concert at age four, far surpassing any musical knowledge which he could have obtained in his first four
years of life. The only plausible cause for such a highly-
developed understanding of music was that it was
worked on for lifetimes and reached its culmination of
expression in that incarnation.

It would be difficult to explain that the talent of
Michaelangelo could be born of one lifetime alone,
never before knowing anything about art.

Those natural talents which you do so well without
having been taught are usually things that you have
worked on before this current incarnation. Consider
the instance of Edgar Cayce, born with the natural
gifts of clairvoyance and ESP. One day as a youngster
he was supposed to read a particular book for his homework, but instead fell asleep on the floor using the
book as a pillow. Upon awakening his father was about
to punish him for failing to do his homework but
young Cayce explained, "I know what's in the book,
I know what it's about."

When his startled father questioned him, young
Cayce was able to answer each question thoroughly
as if he had in fact read every page. Where did this
talent come from?

In the area of phobias that stubbornly resist all
forms of psychiatric treatment, we find the seed of
such extreme fear to be deeply rooted in the soul,
continuing now as a residue, even though the individual
no longer consciously remembers the reason for them.
All it would take to trigger fears of this type is a form
of sensory impression which reminds the individual's
subconscious of a past incarnation, during which time

he may have had adequate reason for the fear. Buried in the soul memory are the negatives of the pictures of every event the individual has ever lived through. All it takes are triggers of light to bring these negatives into focus so that they have the power to affect the individual in his present life.

Without any real understanding of reincarnation much of modern psychology attempts to treat patients suffering from. fear by a process which they call "desensitization." They hope that by desensitizing the individual they will ultimately achieve a state of less reaction to stimuli. Of course, the price to pay is that eventually the patient is desensitized to all stimuli, rather than the select few which pertain to the negatives of his subconscious prior life pain.

When we understand how an individual reacts to time, we have our first clue as to the reason why fears and phobias are so difficult to conquer. It seems reasonable to expect that a way of life perpetuated as a habit for two or three lifetimes could easily take psychologists four or five years of treatment to make any headway with.

In the subconscious desire for a better life, individuals have a strong tendency to compress time. In essence, a chronic problem in a former life which may have lasted thirty or forty years, when triggered in the current life as residue by an event or perception, gets compressed so that the thirty or forty year experience symbolically reoccurs during a relatively short period of time, thereby expanding the emotion of those events to the point that the reaction becomes all out of proportion to the psychologically observable triggers in the current life. At the same time, acute traumas of past lives tend to be so painful in the soul memory that the individual in the current life goes to all extremes to avoid those areas and situations which he subconsciously knows will trigger those negatives. It seems logical that a person who has a fear of height may have fallen to his death in a former life.

From all the cases that I have dealt with, indications show that those qualities, for good or bad, that bear the least amount of integration with the rest of the present life are residue from a past incarnation. Think of every question about yourself that you have never been able to answer. Where do the answers lie?

PART II — THE LAW OF KARMA

Sir Isaac Newton once wrote that "For every action there is an equal and opposite reaction." The great master Buddha teaches us that "You are what you think, having become what you thought." In essence both of these statements are saying the same thing—that for every cause there is an effect.

Therein lies the Law of Karma.

Every thought you have impresses itself into the substance of universal matter where it will ultimately manifest as an effect in the physical world. Sometimes the effect may occur a few moments after the source and then we can readily see how thought and effect are linked together, much the same as throwing a rock into a lake and watching the ripples go out. But at other times the effects go out years after the cause, and it becomes more difficult to see the relationship between the two. And yet always one season follows another. Always summer follows spring. Always the right foot follows the left. Never can a man be going somewhere without coming from somewhere.

Each day is the outgrowth of the day before, as today is the sapling for tomorrow's tree. Each thought is an outgrowth of the thought that precedes it, as each life is another concentric ring in the tree of eternal life. In each incarnation, whatever you do, wherever you go, whatever you think, all you do is meet yourself! And every life experience is to help you refine this self, constantly evolving it to a more perfect expression of your soul.

Such is the law of Karma.

From the Bible we are given the words, "Be not

deceived, God is not mocked . . . . As a man soweth so shall he reap." Those who laugh must learn to cry so that those who cry can learn to laugh. With every tear and smile as you come closer to meeting self, new karma is created for your future.

The soul continually expands its consciousness through its scope of experience until it is ultimately no longer necessary for it to reincarnate into a physical body. Before birth your soul chooses the souls who will become your parents. It defines the religion by which you will live. It selects the neighborhood in which you will be born and reared and ultimately programs into juxtaposition all the life experiences that you will go through, including each blind alley which you will run down until you discover the path of truth.

As your footsteps through life grow lighter, so does your karmic weight. Yet this process of meeting self cannot be rushed for if one stands on tiptoes one is unsteady.

Man is constantly seeking his way home, and he defines his state of happiness by his assuredness of his footing on that path. Wherever man is going he is going home, and his karmic lessons are his roadmap complete with stop signs, obstacles and detours that he must overcome in order to bring his soul to the state of perfection where it can again become one with Pure Spirit.

PART III — LIFE UNDER KARMIC LAW

In his book *Sayings of Yogananda* the great mystic explains reincarnation and karma with these words:

"Master, I am conscious only of the present life. Why have I no conscious recollections of previous incarnations and no foreknowledge of a future existence" a disciple inquired.

The Master answered, "Life is like a great chain in the ocean of God. When a portion of the chain is pulled out of the waters, you see only that small part. The beginning and the end are hidden. In this incarnation you're viewing only one link in the chain of life, the past and the future, though invisible, remain in the deeps of God. He reveals their secrets to who are in tune with Him."

Although most of us have no conscious recollection of former lives, we are not only living the effects of all we have caused in those lives but it is those very causes that initiate us to be born *UNEQUAL!*

We must not confuse the belief that "all men are created equal," with the thought that "all men are born equal." We know that a child born with a birth defect could not possibly expect the same life style or opportunities as a child born without one. A child born in a ghetto could not expect the same experiences as a child born on a country estate. While we do know that the concept that all men are created equal is true insofar as referring to man as a soul entity in his original creation, what he does with that equality from then on as he moves from life to life is completely his own choice and free will. Naturally what he does with this will determine the levels that his soul reaches as well as when he reaches them.

Two different individuals confronted with the same events or circumstances handle themselves differently; one running away from the event and the other coping and rising with it to its highest karmic possibility. The first individual has to repeat the event again and again while the second individual is ready to move on to new lessons. As the days pass into months and years and lifetimes, the second individual will be rising into higher levels of karma more rapidly while the first individual could very easily be dealing with the same basic elemental karmic lessons for an eternity of lifetimes.

Visualize if you will children in a school class at the beginning of the school term. They all start with new books, new clothes, sharpened pencils and new lunchboxes. They all come into the class seemingly equal; however, they have all come out of last year's class unequal. Within a few weeks, some students will have torn notebooks, lost lunch boxes and no homework done, while others will be engaged in extracurricular projects which will bring them higher grades and a great deal of learning and growth during the current school term. When the year is over the same story repeats. Because the students were not equal at the beginning they are less equal at the end. The teacher looking objectively at the class can see the different levels that each student is reaching.

The beginning of the school year is much like the beginning of life; always unequal at the start and always filled with different future lessons for each separate individual.

What's good for the goose is not necessarily good for the gander. As your eyes roam the green valleys of your neighbor's yard, God smiles and says:

"Ah, but I have something better in store for you though you find it not if you try to master your neighbor's lessons."

Although we all live under the same karmic law, we each stand on a different rung of the ladder to perfection. Each step is a different growth phase, the most important of which is the one we are about to take. But always it will be in terms of all the steps we have already taken to get us to the height on the ladder where we now stand. Each of the steps behind us is a past incarnation and in every life we are making sure that all parts of the ladder below us are firm and steady. It is more hazardous to race up a shaky ladder than to struggle on the lower rungs while we make them secure.

CHAPTER TWO

THE ASTROLOGY OF REINCARNATION

PART I — THE TIME LINK

It is generally accepted in the astrological community today that the Nodes of the Moon represent the major key towards understanding your life as part of a continual thread. Many astrologers believe that the Nodes hold more importance than the rest of the chart. To a qualified expert a knowledge of the Sun, Moon and Nodal positions can reveal the entire life of the individual.

At one level these Nodes reveal the track that your soul is running on in the current life, while the rest of the horoscope adds additional information as to how you are to make the journey. It is through the Nodes that Western astrology is now able to make its first inroads into relating this divine science to the Hindu concept of reincarnation.

The Nodes represent the cause and effect relationships by which you lead your life. They are the difference between mundane and spiritual astrology.

Here we find our first clues as to why the rest of the chart is manifesting the way it is. The personality and life of the individual have little meaning if not seen within a larger context. The Nodes place the individual on his stairway to heaven insofar as they define the karmic lessons he has chosen to take on for this life. Therefore his trials and tribulations begin to have new

meaning when viewed as related chapters in the story
of his continuous soul growth.

The individual is no longer apart from the world but
is instead an important part of world evolution. Everything he thinks and does is ultimately a karmic contribution to the improvement of his soul which upon
reaching its ultimate nirvana is an improvement in
the world he has helped to create.

Always man wants to know why. And always he
turns to history for the answer on the assumption that
effect always follows cause. The position of the Nodes
link man with his past and point the way toward his
future. When man can firmly establish the roots of his
past, he starts to experience a thread of continuity
which makes him feel more secure about walking into
his future.

The Nodes are actually points of soul magnetism,
one pulling toward the future and one coming from the
past. The process which we call life is to blend these
two into a median of happiness for the individual, so
that his present incarnation is a symbol of his transition from the past to the future.

PART II — THE SOUTH NODE

The South Node is symbolic of man's past. It is not
symbolic of one past incarnation but rather a combina-
tion of events, ideas, attitudes and thoughts from every
incarnation whose accumulated unresolved effects
have created the current life.

The most deeply ingrained behavior patterns are to
be found here at the point of man's zenith of hundreds
or thousands of years of working on himself. There
is little he could do in the present life to alter greatly
the balance of so many years of training and habits.
For this reason man tends to rest on his South Node
as the comfortable family of his past in whose ways
he is thoroughly familiar. The house he builds for
himself in this life can only rest upon the foundation
he has created before.

For some the South Node can be limiting, while for others whose past foundations are firm and large it can be just the factor which brings the present life to a fruition of achievement.

As an incoming president enters the White House to begin his new life there, so the possibilities of his achievements will be hampered or aided by all he has thought, said and done during his past record in Congress. You are president of your current incarnation but your karmic record in Congress is the concrete steps upon which you stand or the stilts below your wobbly feet.

PART III — THE SOUTH NODE— YOUR ACHILLES HEEL

The potentially weakest spot in any horoscope is the South Node for it represents the footsteps we have left behind us. Regardless of the paths we have taken this South Node trail leaves us open to karmic residue from behind. We constantly look to the future and rarely stop to examine the effects of all we have created until such effects loom ahead of us in our path. Nevertheless, the tracks we have made are still there, symbolizing the habits of lifetimes, and so for many they point the way to the most observable path of least resistance. In fact an individual's most negative traits are those which for hundreds or thousands of years he has allowed to continue brewing within his soul. He keeps trying to piece together the fragments of his deeply-rooted past in the hope that they will form the foundation blocks of his future.

Too often the past itself involves the individual in a type of curious fascination, hypnotizing him back into old methods of behavior, whereupon he forgets the reason for delving into his past and makes his reliving it the actual purpose of his existence rather than the means to the end he originally desired. The South Node can be quicksand; safe enough to look back into as long as no physical steps are taken in that direction. One

step into the South Node is almost certain to immerse
the individual in reliving compressed memories from
which it may well take years and the help of many
other people to pull him back.

It is interesting to note that man's curiosity which is
one of his most formidable assets can also be his greatest enemy, for as tiny flashbacks of his South Node
seep through to his conscious mind his own insatiable
curiosity makes him turn around and go backwards to
seek more. In order to come to full terms with his past,
he seeks more than an intellectual understanding.
Desiring to feel intuitively, relate emotionally, see,
touch and perceive the reality of his past, he inadvertently makes it the reality of his present!

Here without knowing it he has suddenly thrown
himself backwards into another time zone. In essence
he has reprogrammed his computer, but the shift is
so subtle that he doesn't notice it, until the admonitions
of those close to him bring to his sensitivities the
awareness that his functional behavior is somehow inappropriate to the life he is in here and now. Thus the
South Node is to be used as the memory bank of grades
already lived through, but unless there are strong
planetary conjunctions to it, the individual is to move
ahead, forever drawing on his past, but not dwelling in
it.

PART IV — THE NORTH NODE

The North Node is the symbol of the future. It represents a new experience as yet untried. For the individual, this is the new cycle to which he is looking
forward. Carrying with it all the apprehensions of the
unknown and as yet untried experiences, this Nodal
position nevertheless has a curious magnetic allure,
pulling the soul towards its future growth.

There is Divine Providence in trying something
new, and here the individual receives much help for
his efforts. At the very deepest levels of his being he
feels a sense of direction. His purpose to live spurs him

on in spite of all obstacles. In fact, this Nodal position is like a treasure-filled cornucopia reaping one benefit after another as each obstacle is turned into a stepping stone of future growth.

It symbolizes the highest area of expression to be reached in the current life and therefore must be interpreted by the highest qualities of the sign and house in which it is placed. The new experiences seem lonely at first as the individual is unsure of his footing. He soon comes to realize that if his tests of courage are to be meaningful, they must be faced alone at the core of his being where each new adventure finds him as the single character of his own unique experience. The newness of it all creates a peculiar fascination in the individual.

Always he sees it in front of him like the proverbial carrot used to make the donkey walk, yet every time he thinks he reaches it, its higher possibilities become visible to him, demanding still more footsteps, more tests, and more of a desire to go forward. But man cannot reach his North Node until he learns to shed his past for his past represents the shackles of his karmic prison. The new cycle of the North Node is a new problem heretofore unconfronted. It is man's discontent with the old and decaying ways of his past, coupled with his great desire for the discovery and exploration of his higher potential in the future.

With each step closer he starts to feel better about himself. His life takes on new meaning as he experiences possibilities he had never considered. But man does not achieve his North Node until after he rises to the highest karmic levels of his South Node. He must learn to give up gracefully the negative habits and memories which no longer serve a useful purpose in his life. He must be willing to walk where he feels there are no footsteps before him.

The most amazing feature about the North Node is that however much man achieves it, there is always more to go—as it truly represents his everlasting upward spiral towards God.

CHAPTER THREE

THE NODES IN THE SIGNS

ARIES NORTH NODE: LIBRA SOUTH NODE

Here the soul is learning the lessons of self-consciousness on the most elemental levels. Experiences in prior incarnations did not permit the Self to form as a singular identity. Now the individual is paying the price for the indecisiveness of his former lives as well as learning how to rise out of his confusion by developing "one-mindedness."

Highly susceptible to flattery, he goes far out of his way to do the things he believes will please others, but because he has not yet himself gone through ego identification, he becomes confused as to what course of action to take. Always trying to balance those around him, he finds himself to be the eternal referee between two or more opposing ideas, people, or conditions. Standing in the middle, he assumes the role of the buffer trying desperately to bring harmony to both sides at the same time. From moment to moment and day to day, he seesaws from one side to the other, hoping that he will never be required to take a definite stand!

In prior lives he judged his happiness by the successes or failures of those close to him. Now he continues to identify his life through others. His confidence can easily be shattered for he hardly yet knows who he is. By confusing the collective needs of others with his own unrealized desires, he makes himself susceptible to long states of depression. Still, no matter how drained he feels, he continues this past-life pattern of seeking out people with whom he can identify.

At times he develops resentment at his inability to pull the opposite parts within himself together. Yet he is so used to entertaining solutions to contrary ideas that he keeps creating more.

He is attracted to music and the arts, feeling comfortable in an environment that is gracefully delicate. When circumstances around him become coarse or brittle he loses control.

He doesn't like to live alone but desires to be left alone. For his own peace and tranquillity he must learn to overcome his enormous sensitivity to all the disharmonious needs of those around him. He does this best by dropping the attitude that he must fight for his very survival and refocusing his attention on what positive thoughts help him to develop his own identity.

In past incarnations there was great sacrifice to others which was not fully appreciated. Now the soul reincarnates with traces of resentment at not reaping the rewards of its efforts. This brings out the contrariness of the Libra South Node and actually prevents the individual from finding his real Self! The North Node can come out only when the South Node is brought to the highest possible karmic level. Thus, this individual will achieve his greatest potential after he learns to serve willingly, without desiring any rewards beyond his own self-growth.

He was impressionable in other lifetimes. Now he spends at least the first half of this life coping with the leftover residue of his own gullibility. As the years pass he becomes an avid reader, which helps him to crystallize his thoughts. Still, there are so many past-life habits of indecisiveness that he finds it extermely difficult to make concrete decisions.

Always liking to see both sides of everything, he divides himself in half at every crossroad. When these divisions become so painful that he can no longer bear his own indecision, he starts to reach for his Aries North Node.

Ultimately he learns not to be afraid of taking a stand for what his higher Self senses is Truth. He reaches this by teaching himself to be an individual, rather than an extension of somebody else. Still, he must build on his prior incarnations which taught him how to love rather than hate. Thus, as he starts to find himself, he must still be mindful of how his newly-discovered assertiveness influences those close to him.

For short periods of time he will have to isolate himself in order to gather his strength.

His biggest lessons center around learning how to make his head rule his heart for he still melts too easily at the slightest attention.

Of all the zodiac, this individual has the least amount of past-life experience in examining himself. Now he must find out who he really is!

In the current life he is destined to make the transition from the reaper to the sower, whereupon every thought becomes a creative seed for his new beginning.

The house which contains the South Node shows the area in life where too much past identification with others inhibited self-development. The house which contains the North Node designates the area where the Self is now experiencing its birth. Once a new sense of Self-identity is achieved, this individual will feel like Columbus discovering America; and the most amazing part of his discovery is reaching the awareness that it was there all along, but he never knew it.

TAURUS NORTH NODE—SCORPIO SOUTH NODE:

Here the soul is confronted with some of the most difficult karmic lessons in the zodiac. Past lives have been strewn with endings as the Plutonian force of Scorpio worked through its process of transformation.

Now the individual is so frightened by the memory of having the rug constantly pulled out from under his feet that he develops a defensive attitude toward all who offer him regenerative advice. In past incarnations he literally went through the fires of hell to burn away his false values. Now instead of falling back on the remains of Scorpio still within him, he must build through Taurus a new set of substantial values to live by.

Nearly all with these Nodes have at one time touched the force of Witchcraft, and so in the current life there is to be a rude awakening about any remaining residue of the lower Self.

In past incarnations, this individual also had to deal with a powerful sex drive which kept throwing him off balance. As a result, he is used to seeking gratification through all sorts of relationships which ultimately become destructive to the personal ego. Then, confused and embittered by all he sees toppling around him, he is almost glad to aid in the destruction of whatever little remains.

Most of the conditions in this life are still controlled from his subconscious level, buried deeply below the scrutinizing eyes of society. He may appear jovial and friendly, while he is in fact planning some mysterious adventure of intrigue inside.

The chart must be studied carefully to see just how far the soul has come out of Scorpio before an accurate interpretation can be given. For those already closer to Taurus, the violent churning of Scorpio is purposefully avoided at all costs. For those just barely out of Scorpio the internal revolutions are still going on. Planets conjunct either Node will pull the individual toward that Node and literally force him to live through it in the current life.

For all with these Nodes the past residue of revolution is of such powerful intensity that there is bound to be some after-effect spilling over into their present life relationships with family members and close loved ones.

Each day seems to be filled with new emergencies, until one crisis built upon another creates such a turmoil of conflict that the individual is reduced to his most very basic struggle for survival. He doesn't yet know the art of moderation or how to take things at face value for he still believes that others always have an ulterior motive. Inside he feels that he must constantly escape from punishment, and in his escapes he leaves behind him a tornado-like shambles of all he once held dear. At times he sees others turning on him, but rarely does he stop long enough to understand that he is the cause. Whether he is still acting out his past incarnations in Scorpio or advancing through Taurus his fixed stubbornness is very much a part of his ingrained way of doing things.

He will make much growth when he is able to see the actions of others as reflections of his own subconscious!

From past incarnations he has become accustomed to attuning himself to a peculiar brand of intensity, which when not allowed to express itself, turns to anger. He has been deeply scarred with the pain of being hurt, and now like a wounded animal can be deadly to any who represent the slightest threat. On the lower levels of consciousness, individuals with these Nodes can pursue their prey with a personal vendetta. Then when the pieces fall, they appear to be the innocent victims, while they are in fact the carefully planned victors.

Due to the intense emotion constantly seeking expression, a variety of creative outlets are needed.

Sexual desire must be transmuted into Divine Love. All embittering conditions from past incarnations must be dropped from the consciousness until the new seed of peace is discovered. The Scorpio South Node must burn the bridges of the past and resolve to benefit from the lessons of Lot's wife: "Never to look back!"

Through the Taurus North Node he must learn not to dissipate or waste in valueless areas all the power

that flows through him. His greatest achievements in
this life occur when through the development of a great
love for the earth he lives on, he starts to appreciate
glimpses of the source of his unfailing supply and
support. For lifetimes he has misused his energy, his
drives and his desires, feeling himself alone against
all the oppressions and afflictions that affect mankind.
Now through the sensitive impressions of his Taurus
North Node he is to be brought to the awareness that
the abundance in the universe is so great that he will
always have what he needs when he needs it. He must
learn to distinguish the difference between the words
want and *need,* for although he may not always be
able to realize what he wants, he is at every moment
surrounded by all he needs!

As he reaches for his Taurus North Node, he is
reaching at last for stability. He can stop chasing all
he has ever felt cheated of by seeing all that is now of-
fered to him. Ultimately, he is destined in this life to
reach a state of contentment as the seething volcanoes
of Scorpio melt into the blue spirit waters of harmony
in Taurus—where the beloved Gautama Buddha left
his blessing. Truly this is the transition from lifetimes
of war into a garden of peace.

The house position of the South Node indicates the
area in life where any remaining residue of the Scorpionic battles must be conquered, while the house position of the North Node shows the area in life where
the new awareness of trust and security can ultimately
replace the underlying struggles.

*GEMINI NORTH NODE—SAGITTARIUS
SOUTH NODE*

Here the individual receives an invitation to join
society. His soul has come into this life with a past
incarnation residue of wildness. As a result, he is unaccustomed to appreciating the point of view of others.
The karmic continuation of a strong self-righteous

attitude makes it difficult for him to be a fair judge
of his own actions. As such his life is excessive. He is
still attracted to the natural existence without formali-
ties and will go far out of his way to avoid having any
restrictions imposed on him.

He is used to being a free spirit and desperately
tries to retain his sense of liberty at all costs. Whether
married or not, the soul memory of his bachelor-like
attitude makes it impossible for others to get too close
to him.

Believing that actions speak louder than words, he
makes his present life a kaleidoscope of rushed activity.
He always tries to do too many things at a time,
spreading himself so thin that he keeps losing sight of
any central life theme.

In past incarnations he functioned on great reservoirs of nervous energy. Yet, for all his activities, he
has not yet learned how to focus his attention in any one
area. In this life he is still seeking expediency and
finding himself forever the victim of short cuts that
have to be repeated.

Unaccustomed to all the demands of society he
tries to shirk responsibility. He feels that if he can just
clear away all the business at hand as quickly as possible, he will then experience the freedom that society
is trying to take away from him. And so, most of his
time is spent trying to free himself. What he doesn't
realize is that each action creates an equal and opposite
reaction. As a result he is actually making himself
more imprisoned than before.

Always his nature is somewhat primitive. If he is
selfish, it is done innocently. If he steps on others'
toes, it is because he is unaware they are there. Always he seems to miss the obvious, blissfully ignorant
of the immediate circumstances around him. When it
comes to social graces, he is so inexperienced that he
appears to be the proverbial "bull in the china shop."

In the current life, he is learning how to mix with
the society he is benefitting from. Yet, still fearful

of the reactions of people, he lives his life on the rim
of the wheel, occasionally darting into the center of the
hub only to run back out again.

His past life experiences with people were lacking
in the areas of cooperation, sociability and tact. Now
he is striving to reach sophistication. He doesn't yet
know how to see a clear reflection of himself for he
doesn't understand that there are two sides to the same
coin. Through his Gemini North Node, he will now un-
dergo experiences which will force him to see both
sides of every issue.

In this life, he is destined to learn what the world
looks like through the eyes of others. Before he can
understand why people seem not to listen to him, he
must first put himself in their place. Ultimately he will
come to realize that all the negative qualities he has
been attaching to others are things he does not understand in himself.

Sometimes he is a shouter in a library. No matter
how sophisticated he pretends to be, he has so much
past life residue of crudeness in him that it is bound
to seep through at the most inopportune moments.
This embarrasses him so much that he becomes determined to polish himself by paying attention to his
mannerisms, habits, public behavior and particularly
his mode of speaking.

Through his Gemini North Node, he will spend most
of this life's energy learning how to be adept at the
art of communication. He now feels the need to educate
himself, so that he can establish an identity in society.

At one time in the current life he will be faced with
the conflict of whether to live in the city (Gemini) or the
country (Sagittarius). While his basic nature for so
many lifetimes would feel more comfortable in a country setting, he can learn much by adapting himself to
the new experience of coping with city life.

Through his Gemini North Node, he must learn
diplomatically to respect the rights of others if he is
to help preserve a society which in prior lives he

thought unimportant, but in this life is necessary for his very survival.

While his body cries out for sports, nature and the primitive life, his mind will eventually lead him toward a study of words, language and a reflection of his self-expression so that he starts to become a more humanistic part of the culture he lives in.

He is like the wild stallion desperately trying to fight being tamed, and yet wondering what the experience might be like. In the midst of this seeming paradox he is a messenger of the lower and higher minds to all who come in contact with him. His past incarnations brought him to a natural understanding of the universe. Now his mission is not only for himself, but also to spread his understanding to the myriads of people that run through his life. Herein lies the mystical reason for his eternal restlessness. He has much to say and much ground to cover!

The house position of the South Node shows the area in life where past incarnation residue still pulls him toward a desire to be a free spirit. The house position of the Gemii North Node indicates the doorway through which he must walk in order to experience the advantages of the civilized humanistic culture he is destined to join.

CANCER NORTH NODE—CAPRICORN
SOUTH NODE

Here the soul enters the current life with much inner pride. The individual finds it difficult to understand why others do not show him the strong respect he has been accustomed to in past incarnations. As a result, prestige and the pursuit of dignity continue to be the motivators of all actions.

Some with these Nodes will even marry to achieve the social status of the subconscious Capricorn memory.

In past incarnations this soul worked hard for recognition. Without losing self-respect, he would have

been the original ham, going far out of his way to
attract attention. At times this would even mean im-
posing undue punishment upon himself if he knew
others were observing. Now he would like the world to
know how burdened he has been so that others can see
him as a martyr.

He continues to make his work harder than it actually is, never seeming quite able to finish meeting
his current life responsibilities and obligations.

Since he is always living in the past, he has a habit
of bringing the consciousness of all his past burdens
with him into the present. This makes his present life
much heavier than it need be.

The one thing he has not yet learned to tolerate
is failure in himself. He is well practiced at actually
making himself physically or emotionally ill in order to
avoid coping with situations in which he expects to feel
inadequate.

He sees the world through an attitude of self-right-
eousness, whereby the actions of others are rarely
condoned but often condemned. He keeps this to himself, however, for it would damage his sense of personal esteem should others know that he has been
fitting them into his secretly devised caste system.

In prior lives he was highly opinionated and strongly resistant to taking advice that would affect him
personally. Now he still believes that one's personal
life is strictly a private matter. Consequently around
all things which relate directly to himself, he builds
the "Wall of China." It would be futile for anyone
to try to break in for at the slightest personal criti-
cism, he starts adding more bricks to the wall.

Lifetimes of materialism make him an opportunist,
placing himself wherever there is something to be
gained. At the same time he is "penny wise and pound
foolish," for he is known to be stingy in the midst of
emotional bursts of extravagance.

When he sees advantage, he will turn cold and cal-
culating so that no weakness within himself will prevent the attainment of a goal he has his sights on.

He will turn weakness in others to his own advantage. Wherever there are loopholes in the law, he can find ways to squeeze through. So intent is he on managing all he sees around him that his entire current life becomes a personal crusade to prove his worthy capabilities.

In past incarnations, his soul learned the art of accomplishment. In order to do this, there was little regard developed for others. Now through the Cancer North Node, he must learn how to give nourishment as well as receive it. Many with these Nodes experience strong family burdens so that they may come to know the emotional needs of others.

Sexually, the soul is learning how to take on the feminine role in this life. The karmic transition is from coldness to warmth—from age to youth. Many with these Nodes appear to grow younger as each year in their life passes.

Rigid Capricorn attitudes are dropped one by one. The individual finds new security in relating his emotions more honestly. In this life he must learn how to apologize sincerely when he is wrong, as well as not to seek advantage over others when he is right. Eventually he will see that all of his depressions, fears and worries are no more than part of a self-created martyr complex which bears little relation to current life circumstances.

He must slowly learn how to divorce himself from an insatiable need to manage everything around him.

In this life he will go through a chain of experiences which will slowly open up his Cancerian sensitivities. Eventually, he will start to value nature more than money, emotion more than power, and new growth rather than the collecting of dead wood! When the changes start to occur, he will be brought out of the cold of winter into the bright sunlight of early summer. But he must develop a totally new emotional response pattern if he is to adjust to the new direction in which his soul is destined to go.

His highest achievement in this life is nourishing others. To reach this, he must do much work on himself,

until he becomes a natural cornucopia of spiritual food
to those who are hungry. The more he is able to fill
people, the more happiness he will feel himself. He
should see that God also favors those who stand and
wait, and that His highest blessing is especially re-
served for those who seek nothing for themselves but
to be available as His constant servant. In past lives
this soul was able to benefit greatly by receiving.
Now he is here to give.

The house which contains the South Node shows the
area in life in which the bowl of abundance is overfull.
The house which contains the North Node symbolizes
the empty bowls of others waiting for food.

LEO NORTH NODE—AQUARIUS SOUTH NODE

The Leo North Node symbolizes a struggle with
the will. In this incarnation the individual is learning
to develop strength within himself. Conditions force
him to stand alone, very often with the absence of
shoulders to lean on. He eventually learns that if his
life is to be better it must be created by himself. But
before he can build any such creations he must overcome his lackadaisical carefree attitude.

He still continues a past-life tendency to spend too
much time feeling sorry for himself at his lack of
friends when he feels they are needed most. Somehow
in moments of stress, others always seem to be absent.
Long periods of loneliness, isolation and in many cases
a good part of the time spent as a hermit are not un-
common.

Ultimately, when the mind is made up, there is
little that can sway this individual from his destiny.
He must learn that his isolation is a self-imposed
prerequisite for gathering strength. Very capable of
strong leadership in this life, he must learn to overcome all doubts within the self.

The continuance of his past-life desires for friendships actually weaken him, as they do little to build
his individual confidence. He must learn how to be-

come more goal-oriented rather than following his accustomed tendency to dissipate his energies. The interesting thing is that while he continues to think he needs
others to answer his questions, he rarely takes their
advice.

The friends that he does have will be from all walks
of life. In a sense this increases his scope for they
bring to him now the awarenesses that he earned in
former incarnations.

Once determination takes root, there is no stopping
the path towards success for he does not like to settle
for second best. Much thought is given to the future. In
fact he is used to living there, until one day he makes
the realization that "today is yesterday's tomorrow"
and that nothing will exist in the future that is not created now!

He is not the easiest of people to understand, for
he will do anything to retain and emphasize his own
sense of individuality. In past incarnations he developed
a detachment from the majority of the world, allowing
him to feel free to go his own way. Now he takes pride
in being unique and different, caring not as much for
the traditions of society as for whatever rules he has
set up for himself.

His main difficulty in this life is a lack of control.
Without discipline he can generate his power into use-
less projects, until he realizes that nobody will stand
over him with a whip.

If he builds on past-life knowledge, he has a great
ability to do something for the human race for he is
capable of depersonalizing his actions for the good of
all mankind.

Many with these Nodes live a rags to riches life,
the big change coming after the tendency to overlook
is turned into an ability to oversee! Their greatest
amazement occurs when they discover prior-life talents in themselves that they never thought they had.

Happiness is reached once principles are found to
dedicate the life to. Furthermore, these principles must
be unshakable so that the individual feels he is creat-

ing something solid. He will then identify his life in
terms of the size of the principles he has attached himself to.

Disturbed by the scattered activities of others,
which remind him of his own past incarnations, he
feels the strong need to see life moving along a directed
course towards a specified goal. Still, he wants to retain
his complete independence. As a result, he finds it difficult to tolerate others cramping his style. When they
do, they will find him constantly testing limits.

The Aquarius South Node brings with it past life
roots strongly embedded in the principles of fairness
and equality. In the current life, the individual is given
the opportunity to be on his own so that unhampered
by others he may express his intrinsic beliefs. His job
now is to show people as flamboyantly or as powerfully
as he may choose, the ways in which the world can
overcome its burdens. His greatest achievements occur after he has surrendered his personal will to the
service of humanity.

There is no question but that this is good leadership
material so long as the ingrained . past-life Aquarian
sense of fairness is never violated. This individual is
capable of making revolutionary changes in what was
once established tradition. He is first, last and always
amazed and fascinated by all the possibilities man can
reach. At the same time, he is offended when he sees
people pitying their self-imposed limitations, for well
he knows the experience of pulling oneself up by one's
bootstraps.

He aspires to stand tall and not be ridiculed for
those beliefs which he has struggled so hard to express.

While his capabilities for love run deep, the rest of
him is not too far below the surface. The continuation
of his past-life attractions to momentary fascinations
keep throwing him off the track, making it difficult
for him now to see the core of his true self clearly. And
so, he must identify with his achievements as the only
real barometer of his worth.

Though he may at times strongly wish to be alone,

he could never live without people for he thrives on their admiration of his achievements. He believes in firm justice, and yet he is quick to pardon once people have admitted they are wrong. He is never one to strike when a person is down. The sense of fair play has become such a part of his soul that although he feels he should be more competitive, it makes him uncomfortable to be part of any competition which involves foul play.

Things which wouldn't have bothered him in past incarnations suddenly become important as he starts to dig into life rather than disassociate from it. Although it is his present life karma to apply his Uranian ingenuity through practical and traditional Leonian outlets, he still struggles to maintain his unique character.

Some with this position spend the later years of their life alone. Others who are married still hold onto such a strong streak of independence that they tend to keep other family members on the periphery of their circle.

The house position of the South Node indicates the area where past-life needs for originality and freedom are still seeking expression.

The house position of the North Node shows the area through which all the chart energy can be focused into a new shining creation of substantial size and worth, a gift of generosity to the world. Truly these are the Nodes of the "inventor."

VIRGO NORTH NODE—PISCES SOUTH NODE

The object here is crystallization. The individual has to overcome past life superstitions which now impede his growth and see clearly the truth of all things before him. Prior tendencies to be dependent on others as well as to swim in the self-pity of non-achievement are strong obstacles to be dealt with and surpassed in the current life.

The individual must make every attempt not to allow himself to become bewildered amidst the maze

of confusion that clouds his inner vision. Strongly conscious of trying not to hurt other people, much effort
is spent to develop the ability to say what he really feels.
In essence his weak spot is hurting himself, even
though he will have many opportunities in this life to
know better.

He must work to build his confidence, from which
he ultimately learns that nothing happens in his life
until his goals and objectives are clearly defined. In
past incarnations, this individual was deceived by
many through his over-compassionate tendency to fall
for sob stories. Now, he still cringes at the sight of
suffering, strongly feeling the emotion of other people's
pain. He thereby allows external sorrows to drain him
of his strength, until he reaches the point where he's
had enough. Then the realization that his soft heart is
his weak spot pushes him to his Virgo North Node
where he begins to develop the ability to discriminate
between what is truly worthy of his sympathy and what
is indeed fantasy!

He spends much time in the current life sifting
through his value systems, discarding all that is unimportant, so that he may ultimately develop a filter-
ing system which will enable him to make critical
judgments without being swayed emotionally.

This incarnation is to teach him how to swim out
of the pea soup he has fallen into, and what never
ceases to amaze him is the fact that so subtle was his
slipping into illusion that actually he never saw it
happen.

He must try to avoid escapism and daydreaming
at all costs, for in the end these weaken him to the point
that he may forget how to function on the physical
earth plane. From past incarnations his intuition is unusually strong and accurate, but with it comes the
Piscean depressions stemming from a sensitivity to
other people's disappointments.

In learning the karmic lesson of not to depend, he
ultimately discovers that all those he desired to lean
on eventually come to lean on him. He constantly has

to pull out of events, circumstances and relationships whose very heaviness cloud his vision. His own pity for other people can lead him into positions in which he spreads himself too thin. Hating to tell people what they don't wish to hear, he develops the art of subtlety.

One of his biggest lessons in this life is to develop the ability to say no and mean it, for the softest plea from a tear-stained eye has always made him go back on his word. Well he knows his own weaknesses, and it is through this knowledge that he can develop his greatest strength. By the refusal to be swept off his feet by emotion, he gradually swims his way out of confusion.

Many with this Nodal position have been through past-life persecution experiences, and as a result they develop a deep understanding of the pain of others. Still, they can be deceived by others, almost as if their inner gentleness becomes confused with weakness to the point of inviting again in this life the very persecution they are running from.

They have the ability to carry deep hurts within them for many years. Yet from time to time the build-up eats away at their nervous system.

Here the Virgo North Node can act as a savior by cueing them into the diet and health conditions which will bring the most benefit.

These Nodes are especially helpful in the fields of medicine and healing, where the past-life carry-over of a strong compassion for humanity, coupled with a fresh desire for perfection, can be readily expressed. Idealism is high, but the soul's memory of a lack of self-confidence brought about by so much past persecution makes it difficult for the individual actually to believe that he can reach his ideals. He has constantly to fight the tendencies he feels towards giving up. Ultimately it is the great wisdom learned through the bitter lessons of the Pisces South Node that redeem him. For no matter how difficult conditions get, he still clings to his rainbow dream where peace and love rule the world.

He is highly critical of others when he sees them falling short of the perfected ideals he knows they are capable of reaching. He has to learn to put into practical use the essence of his own ideas which he has always vaguely felt but has been unable to verbalize. To the extent that this continues, he feels misunderstood. In times of need he truly wishes for others to help him, yet he feels that it wouldn't be fair to ask for such help. Instead, he keeps seeking out people with depth, silently hoping that they who can see through him will care enough to fathom his problems.

Constantly seeking warmth in others, he turns stone cold when in the company of coarse or crude individuals. One of the most beautiful things about the Pisces South Node is that as the years go by he is afforded the opportunity to develop forgiveness for all those who have hurt him in this life as well as in past incarnations.

These Nodes represent the clouds and the sunshine, the illusion and the real. Always seeking some better state, this individual eventually comes to learn why other people suffer so much. Until he learns this, he goes far out of his way at the risk of hurting himself to help any and all who suffer.

His current life karma is to strive for purification and perfection in himself. while tolerating with gentleness weakness in others. This brings him his biggest lesson—self discipline! He must learn clearly when to let the water run, when to shut it off and when to alter its course.

He must not overlook details for it is often the Piscean lack of attention to detail that causes him to miss the clarity of understanding he is seeking. By developing a clear perspective he can start to avoid the tendency to excess that he has brought with him into this life.

If he is to be happy, his life must be dedicated to service rather than secretly wishing others to drown his past sorrows. His biggest lesson of all is never to doubt the purity of his objectives.

This individual is starting to make things work on the earth plane. In past lives he developed an intuitive understanding of the nature by which man and machine function, but now he is confronted with putting this knowledge to use, rather than daydreaming about some future far-off moment when all his dreams might come true. He must be careful to make all times the present as well as all places here; for only through living in the here and now is he able to funnel into crystalline form the vast reservoirs of essences which he has accumulated through all his lifetimes.

He is to become the focusing lens on a form projector which contains millions upon millions of blurred negatives. Yet through his North Node he is capable of refining each one so that ultimately no knowledge he has ever acquired will be wasted. In effect, this is a rather frugal Node position. Here also the mind and life become as a machine, with all the separate parts forming an integral part of the whole. When any part of the life is not functioning properly, it must be immediately repaired or discarded.

The life is geared to striving to raise efficiency and order out of the sea of the Piscean whirlpool. Much prior life work was spent in renunciation. Now only vague memories remain. In this life, the individual must learn to display the perfected ideals he has achieved through giving up all but his appreciation of the Divine Essence.

The house position of the South Node indicates the area in which a past incarnation reached Cosmic Understanding. The house position of the North Node shows the area through which crystallization can now bring that understanding into material reality.

LIBRA NORTH NODE—ARIES SOUTH NODE

This Nodal position requires much learning about self-sacrifice and the needs of other people. All the lifetimes of work spent on building self-confidence and esteem must now be transferred to others. The Libra North Node keeps the individual from adding to his

sense of self-identity any further. He must guard against
strong ego influencing his current life actions.

His long standing me-first attitude now brings him
sharp and painful experiences as he is learning the
lessons of cooperation. He must slow down and make
sure that all he works for is meaningful, in his marriage and close partnerships as well as all his relations with others. He has to learn to take the sharp
edges out of his life and start to balance. While the
center road seems less attractive to him, it is still the
only path he can have towards happiness.

Ultimately he must learn the very subtle lesson
that his strong pioneering individualism isn't actually
meant for himself at all, but rather to equip him better
so that he can provide others with a more harmonious
life. Many individuals with these Nodes have a tendency to be contrary. The experience of listening to
other people is a new one which they find objectionable
when they feel it hampers their forward motion.

In past incarnations, progress was all important,
and getting there first was part of the highly competitive Arien drive. This carries over into a definite
closed-mindedness which the Libra North Node will ultimately open, showing to the individual the other side
of the coin which he had never before thought was important enough to recognize.

Selfishness and vanity of all sorts must be curbed
unless the individual wishes to find himself alone.
Usually he feels himself being driven towards something, yet he doesn't understand what or why. Through
the Libra North Node he is now to reconsider his goals
and objectives so that his Arian energy is put to some
useful purpose.

He changes his mind often and allegiance to a
single cause is not one of his finer attributes. Past incarnations have made him accustomed to a constant
impatient restlessness that still has a tendency to keep
him on the move. He knows that he is to give rather
than to receive in the current life, yet he finds it difficult to cope with such karma with his full heart.

The Martian quality of the South Node impatiently pushes him in new directions. Upon arrival at each destination, however, he finds the gossamer cloud of Libra in the middle of the seesaw, and is surprised to see that the goal was not a goal at all, nor was the destination the end of the journey. Puzzled and confused, he sits in the middle, trying to evaluate the circumstances which he hopes will point the way towards his next successful drive. And yet each goal, each ambition, each sprint of running and striving brings him to Libra—the half-way point!

Finally, out of sheer exhaustion he makes the amazing realization that the second half of the journey involves other people. He is to learn the karmic lesson that he is not alone. Until he learns to share, something always comes up to put the brakes on his efforts. Eventually he is brought to the realization that winning or losing the game is much less important than the fairness with which it is played.

Many individuals with these Nodes are highly opinionated as a result of selfish or bigoted past-life attitudes. Now it is time for the shoe to be worn on the other foot. Much of the current life's events are painful blows to the ego. The individual has to guard against becoming embittered as he sees many of his own wants and desires being taken away from him and given to others. At first his natural tendency is to be jealous. He wants to fight back for all those things he feels he has lost; yet the more he fights the more he loses. Eventually, drained of much of his inner resources, he must surrender his selfish ego and accept living in a world built on sharing.

Until he overcomes his South Node, his biggest frustration is the witnessing of other people receiving all that he himself had wished for. He doesn't quite yet understand how this works, and is puzzled at why all the things he has ever wanted are coming to people around him and yet not to himself. He hardly realizes that all his desires, wants and wishes are actually designed for others.

He is mentally energizing the wishes of people around him so that he can ultimately be an instrument for their fulfillment. In actuality he is earning himself a new place in the world by living through the karma of selflessness. Still, the insistent urges of the South Node keep pulling him backwards, often making him feel that this is a lesson he would rather not yet learn.

He must try to resist past-life tendencies to make waves for he is now capable of witnessing disharmonies between people without taking sides. Often he is thrown into the position of referee, whereby in helping others to become more objective, he in fact helps himself. The more he can get others to cooperate, the more he can learn to do it himself.

Underneath all the hustle and bustle, this individual is learning to see the consequences of his actions before taking them. In effect, he must learn to look before he leaps!

For many with this Nodal position, there is a deep-seated anger coming out of past-life memories of frustrations which block the self-expression.

In this life, there is usually a very pleasing physical appearance, which is part of the karmic lesson in vanity that the Aries South Node is here to overcome. Any narcissistic residue also causes difficulty in marriage as this is the battleground where the war between love of another and needs of the self must be fought.

The balance between Aries/Mars and Libra/Venus is a difficult one to achieve. The Aries South Node constantly seeks to assert its needs, while the Libra North Node needs nothing for itself but to love others, regardless of their demands. This individual can feel love for others best only after his own needs are fulfilled.

Until the desires of past incarnations are left behind, the incessant pulling of his subconscious demands continues to be so strong that he has a tendency to drain energy from other people, actually putting them to sleep. In effect he is a walking anaesthetic, constantly wondering why people avoid talking with him for more than a few minutes. He would like to talk for hours, if only to continue the focus of attention on himself. But in his private moments, he is deeply saddened by a sense of loneliness and the knowledge that his relationships with others are so far short of what he would like them to be.

There is nothing subtle about this Nodal polarity. Happiness comes only after he is forced to re-evaluate his desires and truly discovers that they involve other people. The ego-self must be abandoned and with it a heightened sensitivity to the needs of others acquired.

The Libra North Node is one of the most difficult to achieve because the Aries self-love looms as such a large hurdle to overcome. Still the individual must overcome if there is to be a new cycle for him, and he will find the key to this new cycle as he begins to reflect back upon himself through the eyes of others.

The house position of the South Node indicates the area where insatiable desires of past incarnations are still demanding priority. The house position of the North Node shows how fulfillment can be reached through self-sacrifice, cooperation and the expression of unselfish love to others.

SCORPIO NORTH NODE—TAURUS SOUTH NODE

Here the individual is learning how to accept revolutionary changes within himself as well as the conditions in his life. He would like to rest, thinking that his soul journey is over. So tired is he, from past life memories of the yoke of his earthly burdens, that whatever the cost he would like to feel settled. As a result, he finds it difficult to develop the strength for future changes.

Tenaciously he clings to old behavior patterns which served him well during past incarnations. He has become personally attached to doing things the hard way. Like the oxen plowing the fields, he walks laboriously through this life as if it were one long straight furrow. He expends so much physical energy that he weakens his Spiritual Self to the point that he becomes blinded from seeing any new possibilities other than the singularly drab existence he has been accustomed to leading.

He finds it difficult to learn by watching others. Instead, he would rather work through each of life's experiences himself. As a result, he spends more time, effort and energy in each growth phase than he has to. Still, he feels he must be sure of himself. So great is his need for security that even when he makes changes in his life, they are in fact not changes at all, but merely other aspects of the same behavior patterns he has been using all along.

In past incarnations he developed a sensitivity to his environment. In order to cope with the continuation of such a sensitivity, he starts early in this life to explore the world of sensory impressions. He learns what feels pleasurable and how to obtain it. Nevertheless, he always seems to fall short of reaching complete and lasting satisfaction. He doesn't realize that one appetite begets another. His great need for possessions makes it difficult for him to enjoy what he does not personally own. As a result, he thrusts himself into long-enduring battles of ownership over people, things and ideas. He stubbornly holds onto all that comes his way. The more he collectively accumulates, the more he traps himself. What was in other lifetimes a great need for the acquiring of substance now turns into the extra weight of excess baggage he is carrying. As the years go by, the yoke of his burdens becomes heavier.

He has created a need to feel powerful so that he can seek temporary refuge from the dismal sense of failure that has plagued him in former incarnations. As a result, he even goes so far as to seek in this life an occupation which puts him in an authoritative position.

He has undergone so much past life damage to the ego that he now experiences an intense need to prove himself worthy of respect. He will fall into deep depression when confronted with the possibility of others finding him lacking in any area. To prevent this from happening, he will push himself towards success no matter what the cost.

It is almost a certainty that at some time in this life the intensity of his karma will bring him to be at least circumstantially involved with the police.

As he reaches for his Scorpio North Node, this individual undergoes a complete transformation. He starts to kill old behavior patterns by burning bridges behind him. Experiences teach him how to cut ties cleanly, so that he does not walk into the future with both feet tied to the past. His biggest growth occurs when he is able to let go.

Inner dependency needs must be transformed into complete independence of thought and action. Strength increases with each passing year as he slowly discards from his consciousness all that oppresses him.

He must learn how objectively to study the results of his subconscious desires so that he can earn self-respect through practicing self-discipline.

These Nodes symbolize the soul who for many lifetimes has been moving along a decadent path. Now the soul vessel is to be turned upside down in order to rid itself of the decay it has collected.

Fulfilling the karma of this overturning process is extremely painful to the individual, as he may lose all he ever held near and dear. In the end, he will unquestionably relinquish more than he bargained for.

So powerful is this transformation that many with these Nodes eventually spend their later years alone. In the process of eliminating excess, they have discarded everything but themselves.

Nevertheless, much of this is necessary if the individual is to reach the point where he can see himself clearly on the very deepest of levels. Out of this symbolic death of all he ever possessed will come his new life.

The house position of the South Node indicates the area which has become decadent as a result of past incarnations. The house position of the North Node

shows the way in which a current-life rebirth can be
accomplished.

SAGITTARIUS NORTH NODE—GEMINI SOUTH NODE

The keyword here is promise. For lifetimes this
individual has enmeshed himself in dualities, resulting
in indecision. He has tried to be all things to all people
and as a result has made himself attuned to super-
ficiality.

Now he has strong karmic lessons to learn in areas
of loyalty and allegiance. Eventually he will come to
see that by playing both sides against the middle he
can only hope to make himself the center of the sand-
wich, caught in the squeeze. Nevertheless he retains
a past-life fear of committing himself fully to either
side for at least on the superficial level, he sees truth
and right in both. He still believes that a definite
commitment to one side would leave him with the
feeling of missing the opportunity inherent in the other.

This ability to remain uncommitted enables him
constantly to adjust himself to fit the needs of the moment. Like the chameleon his colors change with his
surroundings.

In past incarnations he was not too discriminating,
knowing that it really didn't matter where he gave his
affiliations since he never gave his complete self any-
way. Now he swings like a pendulum in the breeze,
open to ride if but for a brief time only on the winning
wind.

He purposely makes himself the pawn of others
and, even if only for the moment, seems to agree with
them so that he can temporarily feel accepted and a
part of something.

Through many lives his sense of self-identity has
become not merely a single division but filled with all
the questions of everybody he was in contact with.
Since so many people have formed the building blocks
of this inner self, it is impossible for him to be anything but a hypocrite!

When he speaks his facial expression as well as body language will change from sentence to sentence, taking on the appearance of the person whose words he is now trying to pass off as his own. In fact, when he makes a definite positive statement, his eyes will always examine the recipient to see if it was received as truth. If not, then it doesn't matter for he will now start talking incessantly, trying one collected statement after another on for size in the hope that somewhere in his collection of information a few words might be worthwhile.

He loves activity, and when circumstances make him feel cooped up or bogged down he becomes highly nervous and restless.

Always over-programmed, he struggles to keep up with the myriad of details and people that fill his life. He has so much to do and yet at the end of each day feels distracted from his purpose.

In past incarnations he never developed a long attention span. As a result, he spends much of this life constantly changing his mind about everything.

At one point, he will go through conflict. over whether to live in a large city or in the country. The conflict is really between the continuation of his past-life need to be with people and his present-life desire to be away from them.

Direction does not come at an early age. More often than not, it comes through the aid of parents or an older person who sets him on his course. This occurs usually after age twenty-eight.

Underneath it all he is unsteady; he has been so busy seeing the shades of gray in everything that he has difficulty seeing the light of truth in himself.

For this individual, life's biggest task involves a quest for higher knowledge. Through the Sagittarius North Node he must learn that in order for man to be capable of seeing the truth, he must first be the truth!

He will go far if he teaches himself to speak from his higher mind for the esoteric meaning of all he says will ultimately show him his real identity.

When he starts to mesh with Transcendental Thought, he will begin to reach a spiritual union within himself.

First he must work through his karma of perpetuating trivia and come to see that participating in gossip is the greatest sin against liberty. Then he must turn his back on all the past-life residue of pretended sophistication and reach for all that is *real* and *natural*. Ultimately, he comes to see that although a coin has two sides, it's still one coin! When he develops this perspective of vision, he will be able to transform the knowledge he has acquired into Divine Wisdom.

The house position of the South Node shows the area where past incarnation personality conflicts still plague the lower mind. The house position of the North Node shows the ways in which a Higher Consciousness can be developed into a vehicle which enables him to rise above all conflict.

His present-life evolution will free him from the bondage of indecision and in its place give him glimpses of Universal Truth.

CAPRICORN NORTH NODE—CANCER SOUTH NODE

This individual is learning how to achieve maturity. In past incarnations he had a tendency to look at life through rose-colored glasses, seeing only what he wanted to see with a definite conviction that everything else didn't exist.

Now there is still much of the "baby" left in his Cancer South Node. He is so used to going through his prior lives on crutches, wrestling with his dependencies while seeking bannisters to lean on, that his current life is the resultant shambles of escapist, childlike habits which keep impeding his growth.

Truly, this is the perennial infant, desiring at all costs to maintain his role as the focus of parental attention. In areas of problem solving, he would rather have his parents do it. Everybody he meets and knows, be it friend, business associate or marriage partner, automatically becomes the symbolic parent to pick up the pieces of his misery, protecting him from being hit by the falling sky which he has created. He even creates his own self-inflicted illnesses if they bring with them the slightest hint of gaining love and affection.

Constantly practicing at becoming an adult he seems never quite ready or willing to make the transition fully. Somehow he keeps feeling he needs much more practice first.

All he does in this life is based on his soul memory of sensitive past-life feelings which still are shattered by the slightest rejection.

Many individuals with these Nodes are strongly wrapped up in the business of their country. They personalize government for to them it is still part, in a larger sense, of their own Cancerian family.

Underneath all else there are unusually strong feelings of patriotism and loyalty.

Many with these Nodes focus a good part of their strength and attention on younger people.

They like to listen to the trials and tribulations of others, but not being quick problem solvers themselves, they have a tendency to hold everything inside them. As the weight of problems increases, like collecting layers, they seem to age in spite of themselves.

The most difficult karmic problem of the Cancer South Node is learning how to let go. The individual brings with him into this life such strong inner fears of ever losing or forgetting anything that he keeps making extra special efforts to retain all he has ever gone through. As such he makes himself the "psychic garbage pail" of the past. Constantly he is thinking about his present in terms of what he should have done years ago—or "lives ago." He often can be seen sorting through old photographs hoping to create his future out of fragments of his past.

At times he is extremely draining, using whatever is done for him as a springboard to ask for more. He tries other people's patience with all of his emotional problems, and long after the solutions are given to him he refuses to see logic through his cloud of emotion. He is not so much interested in finding out why something went wrong as he is seeking the lost feeling to be returned.

Endings are especially difficult for him to deal with. The word "good-by" has never been a part of his vocabulary for he has always tried to preserve all relationships as long as possible. His behavior in regard to objects is no different, since he tends to form permanent attachments to the nostaligic memories they carry with them.

The major karmic lesson in the Capricorn North Node is to identify with an ideal bigger than the personal life. The individual must ultimately come to stand for something, in spite of all his real or imagined personal difficulties. He must understand true responsibility.

Many with these Nodes eventually become self-appointed hallmarks of tradition. They would rather die than have an outsider know any part of their personal life which contradicts the principle they have chosen to stand for.

Through the North Node an image is established which others can look up to and model their lives after. At times personal difficulties deplete him of the strength to hold up this image, and yet hold it up he must, even if it means sacrificing his entire life. In most of his endeavors he is capable of becoming a methodical and cautious planner once he learns to overcome his past-life tendency to overreact emotionally.

In the charts of females, these Nodes represent an unusually strong search for a father figure. In males, there is a strong consciousness of the need to fulfill the father role.

The most important thing about the Capricorn North Node is that it represents the point through which the individual will meet his karmic mission. For this reason alone, many with these Nodes tend to be reluctant to accept the full concept of adulthood. They would prefer to remain in an immature state for as long as possible for they sense a type of judgment awaiting them. Much like the condemned man desiring one stay of execution after another, they seek to hide behind others, constantly pushing themselves further and further to the back of the line so as to avoid meeting the effects of all they have created. This is the reason why many of them have great difficulty in accepting their own chronological age. While they admit to their age openly, they try not to live it.

There is much past-life residue of immaturity. The soul has become fixated at one point in early growth. Now there is great difficulty passing that point. Still, it will be passed, if the individual is ultimately to stand for something.

The zodiacal constellation of Capricorn is the gateway through which the soul must go upon leaving the physical body, and in this most occult of signs it will stand for inspection before the Judges at these Gates. While this may not be the last incarnation on earth, it will most definitely by house position receive karmic judgment in one area of the life. The individual with these Cancer-Capricorn Nodes will flounder half his life in helpless abandon and then one day resign himself to stand up to the saying, "T'is a far, far better thing I do than I have ever done before."

The house position of the South Node indicates the area in which the karmic residue of immaturity seeps into the current life. The house position of the North Node shows the ways in which the individual can now enter responsible adulthood by aligning his life with the principles of honor, respect and tradition.

As soon as he learns how to do this, he is destined for a life of splendid accomplishment.

AQUARIUS NORTH NODE—LEO SOUTH NODE

These Nodes represent the struggle between the personal life and an impersonal dedication to humanity.

The Leo South Node symbolizes prior lives where much revolved around the self. The North Node in Aquarius points to a future of service for mankind, where the individual will assume the role of the "Waterbearer," so that he may be an instrument in the crusade for world evolution. Before he can do this, the enormous power of the Leo South Node must be dealt with.

From past incarnations he has a tendency to look down on other people and to be condescending of their thoughts and ideas. There is an intense pride which leads him toward name-dropping, as well as designing his life so that he is seen and known to be in the company of special people. He separates between royalty and the common man, setting himself or others close to him on pedestals. Seeing himself as the central point of the universe, he views his powerful will as the means of obtaining his ends, rather than adjusting to a fair acceptance of life.

His karma now is to learn how to walk lightly, without leaving footsteps, for in essence he is the ruler making ready to abdicate his throne.

Constantly his past-life ego rears its ugly head, preventing him from achieving the very happiness he seeks.

These Nodes cause great difficulties in marriage for the individual experiences a strong tendency to dominate those close to him. When he can't do this, he becomes a complete hermit, freeing himself of all responsibility out of sheer disgust.

While he asks others for advice, he still must do things his own way.

His biggest conflicts center around what is artificial and what is real. There is so much martyr-like romanticism in his Leo South Node that he finds it easy to slip into the role of Don Quixote chasing windmills!

He must learn how to shed masks, ultimately discovering that ego-centered displays of dignity are coming from past-life habits and do very little now toward bringing him any lasting happiness.

For those whom he does hold near and dear, he is

highly protective, and yet he has a strange tendency to wander, finding on his journeys many of the waifs and strays of society. In these outermost regions where society overlooks its existential possibilities, he discovers new horizons to explore and conquer.

He is destined to spend part of his life alone for his unique character is too overbearing to be readily acceptable by most people. Although he enjoys having others recognize and applaud his grandiose achievements, he cannot stoop to chase people. His soul remembers a sense of pride which now forbids him to compromise his dignity.

If given the right cause, he will sacrifice his entire life for it. It is not the sympathy of others that interests him so much as their admiration for his glorious deeds.

He is repulsed by mediocrity, seeing it as a threat to his ever-present drive to reach the top, to burst the bubble, to grab for the brass ring.

If he is of the negative type, he may even use people to achieve his ends. Friends, neighbors and relatives become stepping stones on the rungs of his success ladder.

Through the Aquarius North Node he learns to overcome his past-life sense of prestige and develops the concept of Universal Brotherhood. He must ultimately come to see himself as part of a larger cosmic sphere, in which his role is to share in the burden of human evolution. He will reach his greatest happiness when he is able to set aside his own needs and substitute in their place a new humanitarian attitude toward all he sees around him.

He is to forget pride and reach for new original horizons, no matter how eccentric his ideas seem to others. Through his North Node he is given the promise of a unique adventure, through which he can make an important contribution to the progress of civilization.

The house position of the South Node indicates the area in life that is too burdened with the desire for personal achievement. The house position of the North Node shows how the individual can set himself free

from the shackles of his past-life ego by realizing the
mission for humanity for which he is destined to pick
up his cross.

PISCES NORTH NODE—VIRGO SOUTH NODE   *LSC*

In the realm of consciousness, this is the hardest
Nodal position to deal with. Here, as a result of many
lifetimes, the individual starts to realize his own ri-
gidity. He is aware of his patterns and how much they
hurt him; yet he finds them difficult to let go of. In
prior lives, he lived in the consciousness of a finite
universe where all was well structured. Now he is
confronted with the realization that truth extends beyond what his finite senses can measure or even perceive.

He is unavoidably confronted with situations, circumstances and events which force him to relinquish
his hold on the physical plane. Nevertheless he still
tries to live like the salmon—swimming against the
current, regardless of the direction of nature's forces.

He still seeks order. In fact, his need for strict
regimentation is so strong that he develops medical
troubles in the center of the body from personalizing
a stiffness that increases tension on the inner organs.
Constantly he suppresses desire for the sake of doing
what seems proper for he would like to maintain an
image of respectability.

In past incarnations he built his understanding on
fact, not hearsay. Now he accepts only what comes
from the "highest authority."

He seeks ways to rid himself of the nervous irrita-
bility which keeps overcoming him, and yet he puts
stipulations on the cure.

He must learn how to immerse himself in the
waters of Cosmic Consciousness, and in this baptism
of thought he can truly experience a new birth. Before
he can do this, however, he must first overcome his
karmic fear of living in a contaminated world.

He comes into this life believing that the world is

filled with danger, and therefore constantly questions the credentials of the people and conditions he considers allowing into his life. Everything foreign to the self represents the threat of disease, and it is because of such thinking that from time to time disease actually occurs.

For many with these Nodes there is strong residue of sexual problems left over from former incarnations. Either a deprivation of the sexual experience, or a strong determination to avoid emotional hurt through it, leads them to seek a better understanding in the current life. Some are confirmed Puritans, while others are capable of being physically responsive and emotionally cold at the same time.

The mind is so analytical that life can easily slip into the manipulation of a chess game. This individual has a sharp eye for detail and never overlooks the obvious. He is an expert at solving puzzles, willing to spend many hours tediously groping for the tiniest answer, but he can get so involved with whatever he is doing that he often loses perspective. His past-life discriminating tendencies often lead him now to pick apart what should be left together. Thus, although he is capable of immense clarity of thought, he does not experience complete peace of mind.

Through the Pisces North Node, he must learn Faith. When he stops separating the world into neat little compartments, he will get his first glimpses of Universal Consciousness. Ultimately he is to achieve the understanding that all is one, and one is all. Before this happens, he must learn how to stop seeing himself as separate from the rest of the world.

He will go through experiences which force him to grow more compassionate.

As he starts to find his well-laid plans dissolving into nothing, he begins to see others in a different light. Ultimately he symbolically goes through the pain of the entire universe so that he can strengthen his Divine Love to the point that he absolutely refuses to pass judgment on others.

He makes much progress by acquainting himself with the spiritual way of life. His growth extends as far as his arms can reach. While the arm of the past still clutches at his self-imposed restrictions, the arm of his future is grasping for the higher alternative. It is only his failure to let go completely that prevents him from achieving the perfect transition into the full state of higher mind. Yet, he does reach the point that he occasionally sees it.

From time to time his remarkable intuition reveals to him the mysterious essence of life, yet the past incarnation memories of his Virgoan practicality cause doubt at every point. And so, half way between one world and another, these mutable Nodes are in a constant state of change.

Arriving at his destination but not sure that he is there, he keeps going back to start his journey again. Each time he reaches one step more into the infinite, where ultimately he will dissolve the shackles of his rigidly formed past and be born again as pure Sprit.

The house position of the South Node indicates the area in life that is still too rigidly embedded in a personally overstructured idea. The house position of the North Node shows how the soul can renounce its grip on all rigid definition of form and structure so that it can be free to swim in the Ocean of God.

CHAPTER FOUR

THE NODES THROUGH THE HOUSES

FIRST HOUSE NORTH NODE—SEVENTH HOUSE SOUTH NODE

This individual is here to go through experiences which challenge the self. In former incarnations he fell into the trap of depending upon undependable people.

Spending too much time trying to help others understand themselves, he never stopped to reflect on how their same situations and circumstances played an important role in his own identity. As a result of putting the accent outside the self, it now. becomes difficult for him to see who he really is. This is particularly strong if Neptune is found near the Ascendant.

These Nodes indicate past incarnations in which the individual submerged his identity in the affairs of others. Marriage and partnerships are so deeply rooted in his way of doing things that his quest of self is constantly viewed through other people's eyes. He therefore allows their thoughts and opinions of him to influence his own sense of identity.

Ultimately he must come out of the bondage of trying to be all things to all people and in the light of his own singular vibration, establish who he really is. He must escape from living in the shadow of other people's lives.

His soul memories of cooperation and teamwork

are so strong that every time he falls back on them, he actually extinguishes himself in the causes of others.

His first house North Node now brings to him the awareness that somehow he has lost his identity. Submerged in the desire to please, he has made himself a reflection of an ideal peculiarly opposite to his own basic nature. This causes him much current-life pain as he desires to come out of himself while at the same time not inflict hurt upon those near him.

He must ultimately learn how to assume gracefully the role of leadership. This is extremely difficult, because he has had so much prior-life experience in being submissive. He has sacrificed himself so that others could achieve their goals.

All of his important experiences revolved around docile acquiescence. Now the highest growth potential is to establish a sense of self without shutting off completely the benefits of marriage and partnerships. Too often when he becomes aware of all he has sacrificed through his South Node, he becomes an extremist, feeling that one state of existence inhibits the other. He starts focusing every part of the life energy around the desire to lead rather than to be led. Through an instinctive knowledge that his Achilles heel or weak spot is in the ways that he can allow himself to be put into the position of being taken advantage of in marriage, he develops the tendency to become too over-assertive. He tries too hard to make up for what he feels he has lost.

To achieve happiness in the current life, he must learn how to balance equally his own needs with those around him. He must deliberately try not to rush his own growth and independence, with the understanding that the most beautiful flower takes time to blossom, while only the weed grows quickly!

The sign which contains the South Node indicates the ways in which the individual during former incarnations submerged himself in others. The sign which contains the North Node shows the ways in which he can now establish his own sense of identity.

LSC

SECOND HOUSE NORTH NODE—EIGHTH HOUSE SOUTH NODE

The individual with these Nodes spends a good amount of his current-life energies on the darker side of life. From past incarnations he has secrets which he now spends most of his time guarding carefully. His greatest difficulty is in attempting to lead a life which is beyond reproach for his lower self is powerfully strong.

He desires light, but with every step he takes toward it the aching of his guilt-ridden subconscious blocks the road.

He has had much prior-life experience behind closed doors, where the eyes of open society failed to look. He is even accustomed to creating deceitful circumstances where there were none before.

Actually, he is testing the limits of other people's values, and while many may know him closely, none will know him well.

Inside, he is highly nervous for fear of others unlocking his secret doors; for well he knows that he is undermining nearly everything he touches. Yet he has the self-assuredness to believe that all will go well no matter where his sometimes immoral adventures continue to lead him.

Because this individual has not yet established his own sense of values, he tries desperately to study the values of others. In so doing, he inadvertently pushes others off their track and therefore can be a threat to all that others hold near and dear. In former incarnations he destroyed much of his own value systems, so now he finds it difficult to understand why others cherish the things they do. He doesn't have his own stake in this life, so with nothing to lose he feels free to claim-jump the stakes of others. Usually, this is accomplished in such subtle fashion that it is extremely difficult to recognize.

There is also strong past-life residue of sexual misuse. He has learned to think of his sexuality as his strength, using it as foothold to gain possession of others. In the female, this is the story of Delilah or Mata Hari, whose unusual sexual powers lured the strongest of men from their appointed missions. In the male, much of the life energy is dissipated on sexual thoughts. He doesn't use it for power in the same sense as the female, but it is for him the reassurance that all is going well with his ego.

The interesting thing is that sex is never the end but always the means. In the give and take barter system, sexual allure or responsiveness becomes the payment in exchange for another's values.

Individuals with these Nodes become jealous easily. Constantly they wish to trade places with whoever seems to have a greener backyard, and all too often they feel that sex is a fair price to pay for all the honors they may eventually receive.

From past incarnations, this individual feels shunned by society. Now, on the outskirts of acceptance, he is like a little lost child in the winter snow, peeking into the window of a brightly lit cabin with the hope that somebody will come and let him in out of the night.

He is less than discriminating, for he desires such an immediate release from his current pain that it hardly matters to him whether he is jumping from the frying pan into the fire.

He turns to wherever solace is available for his loyalties have not yet reached the state of evolution that they may be considered totally trustworthy.

In his current-life childhood, he experiences fear of death, almost as if death itself would be the logical punishment for all his misdeeds in past incarnations.

He keeps feeling that he has to fight for the things he needs for he has no sense of having yet earned them. When he falls short of reaching the brighter side of life, he secretly blames others for his misfortunes.

In a few rare cases this individual must overcome past life criminal tendencies or residue of witchcraft. Only through a proper assessment of his second house North Node can he establish the substance that will lead to a new rebirth.

Here the memory of past lives has to be brought to the surface and then eliminated completely in this eighth house of death before the soul can progress into a new set of values.

The individual must learn to develop and build that which is sincerely meaningful to him, understanding clearly that that which is dishonorably obtained is highly difficult to preserve. He cannot expect to grow through other people's efforts for if he wishes to cross the bridge, he must pay the toll out of his own pocket.

As soon as he grows to this realization, the lighted cabin door swings open for him; not through the goodness of others, but because he has earned it!

The sign which contains the South Node indicates the ways in which former incarnations have brought the individual to be too preoccupied with the business of others.

The sign which contains the North Node shows the ways in which he can now build a substantially new and meaningful life for himself by establishing his own value systems.

THIRD HOUSE NORTH NODE—NINTH HOUSE SOUTH NODE

These Nodes represent a karma in relationships. The individual is here to learn how to fit the intertwinings of people and ideas into the scope of his understanding.

The ninth house South Node shows an accent on growth in former lives. Literally millions of hours of thought were spent on developing an abundance of wisdom. Much was sacrificed to do this, particularly the enjoyment of meaningful relationships with others. So that a large amount of soul growth could be accomplished, a freedom to explore without restriction or limitation had to be developed first.

Now in the current life the individual is habitually linked to his past incarnation sense of freedom, which although he feels he must retain, he can no longer consciously remember why.

From time to time he feels a wanderlust to visit different horizons for somewhere off in the distance is the rainbow he is used to seeking. He is a mental nomad, constantly travelling through the great expanse of his consciousness, stopping only for rest at each oasis which offers temporary shelter from his restless urge.

Always he is seeking yet it is difficult for him to define exactly what he is looking for. He finds others puzzling as he curiously tries to understand what makes them tick. Herein are some of his major karmic lessons. He must learn how to interact with people. Though he may be happily married or involved in close relationships, he still retains a sense of bachelorhood in his thoughts. He must learn how to make his life fit into the exact puzzle slot allowed by all the other lives around him.

The ways in which he relates and communicates will constantly be put through one test after another. Ultimately he will find himself enmeshed in a network of people, so that all the knowledge he has acquired in previous lifetimes can be put to practical use.

In his current-life relationships, he feels frustrated with not enough room to move. This enclosure of people around him eventually comes to extinguish his past-life tendencies to be vague and evasive and in its place teaches him the art of pinpoint communication.

He is very much concerned with the values of sexuality, feeling obliged to conquer any grip this force has on him. Now he sees clearly the presence of a higher and a lower self, and it is the pull from both which he must karmically wrestle out.

The individual is less concerned with gain than with protection against loss. He is terribly fearful of losing the freedom he was accustomed to in past incarnations; yet he must risk such loss if he is to interact with humanity. As soon as he is willing to take this risk, he is ready to receive his greatest rewards.

Ultimately he elevates himself through reading and purposeful study, and although he is more used to informal ways of learning, it will be a formal education that now puts it all together for him.

This Nodal position often causes a friction marriage, since the individual is prone to seeking out-of-wedlock relationships in which to work out the understanding of personality interactions that he must develop.

One of his biggest lessons is to learn how to consolidate his energies for each time he feels the urgency to move on with things, he tends to leave loose ends scattered behind him.

His life is wide in scope, not only in areas of knowledge, but also in the myriad of people he meets, and the multitude of places he travels.

He will ultimately be known as a Messenger, bringing to all those who need it the specific bits of information that like manna from heaven are placed in their lap at the moment of hunger.

In essence, he is a teacher's teacher for although he has little patience with a classroom situation, he is well capable of feeding information wherever and whenever it's needed. He likes doing this because it fulfills his past-life need for movement. As such he never gets a chance to see how important the information he is disseminating actually is. Nevertheless he has an enormous effect on the awareness of all those whose lives he touches.

His own life is as interesting and full as an encyclopedia, for he tries to live much of what he reads about.

For all of his movement one would think him desirous of having a rest, but underneath he is highly nervous and needs this amount of movement in his life. The nervousness is not to be considered a negative trait, but rather as part of his mission. It reminds him that he has a task to do. Every moment a piece of information comes into his mind the nervousness gets triggered, reminding him that he must deliver it somewhere.

In past incarnations he avoided conclusions. Now he refuses to make a final judgment on anything. This is part of his understanding that if he were to make a

final decision it would be premature for he knows that
new information will constantly be coming.

He is superficially conversant in almost all areas.
Still, on the personal plane he is highly misunderstood,
for the messages he delivers are so uniquely disguised
that they have a tendency to go over the heads of
others who only see him as eternally gossiping about
nothing.

The truth is that all of his words are important, but
they must be seen to have deeper than surface value
before they can be interpreted properly. He is truly
the fast-winged messenger of the gods.

The sign which contains the South Node indicates
the unintelligible ways in which the independent higher
mind is accustomed to receiving its coded information.
The sign which contains the North Node shows the ways
in which the individual can now translate his knowledge into a language which society can understand and
accept.

*FOURTH HOUSE NORTH NODE—TENTH
HOUSE SOUTH NODE*

This individual must learn to overcome the karmic
feeling that he is the vital center of all situations
around him.

He comes into the current life with subconscious
memories of a past sense of dignity, which leads him
to believe that at least certain areas of life experience
are beneath him.

His prior incarnations have put him in the position
of being captain of his own ship, if not the commander
of others. As a result, he is used to assuming an authoritative position whenever the weakness of others triggers his powerful need to take charge.

He enjoys the role of protector and goes to extremes in filling his life with those whose very weaknesses put them under his dominion. By so doing, he
is constantly testing his own power to stand tall.

This is a lonely position for here the individual is so concerned with his self-appointed mission that he never allows others to see into his real self underneath. What he shows is a facade or the uniform of the role he feels obliged to play.

In the current life he goes through experiences which teach him to come down off his skyscraper and make sure of the foundation underneath.

It is in the area of his most highly intimate relationships within his own family that the stage is set for his lifelong battle in an attempt to gain control of his own roots.

Many with these Nodes have one unusually demanding parent whose expectations encourage them to believe that they are truly destined to achieve a position of sitting on top of the world. As a result, they are discontented with whatever situation they are in, for always it falls short of what they feel they were meant to do.

The karmic lesson here is that "A bird in the hand is worth two in the bush." The individual must overcome his readiness to forsake what he has for the possibility of attaining what he doesn't.

So unwilling is he to see himself in a back-seat position that when circumstances force him to do so he may in extreme cases even contemplate suicide; for he firmly believes that without achieving some great destiny, life is utterly worthless.

This incarnation brings him through the experience of facing the conflict between a career for himself and the demands of his family.

He must learn maturity for with all his projected strength, power and dignity he is nearly a cripple when it comes to solving his own emotional problems. He must examine his roots and after pulling his head out of the clouds of his past, build a practical foundation for his future.

Eventually he learns that his organizing for others is merely a distraction from putting his own life in order.

The relationship established with parents early in life is more important in these Nodes than in any other position of the zodiac. Here the individual will spend much of his life energy attempting to be totally free and independent of his parents, yet always conscious of how much he needs them. Nevertheless, the reaction patterns to life continue to show a definite parental defiance, masking a strong need for parental love.

This soul is at a point in karma where he feels unappreciated for all his efforts. The past incarnation residue is based on achievement for the sake of recognition and appreciation. Now, achievement is to be its own reward. The soul must stop trying to gain audience for its deeds, realizing that the audience will always be there if the deeds are great enough. It is in this process of seeking an audience through which the individual tends to lose himself. He must literally transform his fourth house into a new birth of emotional attitudes, learning the lessons that when a man stands on tiptoes he is unsteady.

His life is like the beautiful orchid: a splendid sight to behold when raised and nourished under the most delicately controlled environmental conditions, but once the orchid is prepared for display, it is snipped from its roots, insuring wilting and certain death after a short time. This individual will be faced with the choice of being the overlooked orchid growing in a garden of thousands, or sacrificing his own happiness to be the beautiful flower on someone's lapel. As soon as he overcomes his past-life need for display, he can start to grow to the maturity he is so desperately seeking.

The sign which contains the South Node indicates the ways through which he still overemphasizes his importance. The sign which contains the North Node shows how he can grow to become in substance so emotionally fulfilled that he no longer has to equate his happiness with his soul memory of prior-life personal esteem.

FIFTH HOUSE NORTH NODE—ELEVENTH HOUSE SOUTH NODE

Here the individual is learning about the Creative Process. He spends much time in the clouds, hitching his wagon to some distant dream or pondering through his vast multitude of fantastic ideas. In past incarnations he lived for the fulfillment of wishes. Now his gossamer world of wispy dreams is so ornamented with the accumulated fragrance of promise that it takes a great deal of realistic prodding to shake him loose.

From a young age he has learned to become a "people-watcher," spending most of his conscious hours pondering the possibilities of other people's actions. As a result of prior lives, he has learned to become highly imaginative and inventive; at times he is even ingenious, but he is too used to spending most of his mental powers working out the intricate plots of his fantastic daydreams.

He never ceases to amaze himself at the oddities he can conjure up within his own mind, but for all his ingenuity he is one of the least practical people of the zodiac. He is always deeply enmeshed in thought. What he is really doing is seeking symbols which will provide new material for future dreams.

His karma is to learn the importance of dreams, inasmuch as how they explain his life. Ultimately he comes to realize that his entire existence has consisted of acting out his dreams, to the point that he has become the puppet of his own fantasies.

When he does come down to earth, his first instinct is to reach for friends who in either appearance or behavior remind him of the characters of his wispy fantasyland.

His mind is constantly drifting off into the distant future, and there, in the science fiction of a century as yet unlived, he indulges himself in the intriguing fascination of the remotest possibilities which would otherwise have little or no bearing on his current life. Still he likes to ponder.

He thinks much about the value of his work as
well as of the effects of his childhood, both of which he
blames for his difficulties in coping with his sex urges.

The truth is that neither his work nor his parents
nor even his sex urges truly bother him, but instead
his frustration arises from the gap he sees between
the reality of his past-life dream world and the sharp
awakening circumstances through whose boundaries
and limitations his current life is actually lived.

He finds it difficult to understand why there is a
barrier between dreams and actions and as a result
he spends much effort trying to break through the walls
of limitation that separate one world from the other.

But all the while he is dissipating his strength, and
the more he does this, the less he is able to create his
own life.

He must realize that through his fifth house North
Node he is now given the greatest gift that man can
receive—the power to create his own destiny. By study-
ing the process of creation, he can become aware that it
is his own thoughts that have caused all the circumstances that he deems real in his life. He must then go
further to understand the link between his thought and
his dreams, for truly it is his life of dreams that in
greater measure than he thinks is creating his life on
earth.

He must learn to be responsible about his dreams
and careful of what he wishes for since he, more than
one with any other Nodal position in the zodiac, will
actually see his dreams materialize. But always the
physical effect of each dream comes with a slight
twist; enough to make him aware of the danger of
creating selfishly.

This individual will have to live his dreams long
after he remembers the reasons for them. It is a strong
part of his continuing karma to understand "wish
power," and how better can he understand it than by
living through the consequences of all his wishes.

Thus, his life is both a blessing and a curse for
each time he rubs Aladdin's lamp his soul will either

move higher on the wings of spirit or sink miserably in the depths of his own private hell.

He is learning that the dreams of his eleventh house South Node are under the rulership of Aquarius where they must be dedicated towards a service for humanity and that the more he wishes for others the more he will ultimately have for himself. But when he reverses this process his life becomes a veritable shambles.

If he chooses to create for himself, he faces the unfortunate results of misusing a sacred gift for his dreams ultimately will become so jaded as to be utterly worthless insofar as they are able to bring him happiness.

Unless these Nodes fall in water and earth signs they can cause difficulty in relationships and marriage due to so much past-life residue of non-attachment.

Major turning points in the current life revolve around children, through whose eyes the individual comes to understand his own sense of self-worth. He observes how children put their dreams into action and soon comes to realize that instead of making his dreams the plans for his future he actually has been allowing them to block every present moment. Once he sees his dreams as a well with no bottom, he is able to let go of the castles in the sky and focus his attention on whatever he is creating in the present.

To do this he even reaches the point of becoming aware of how he allows his great need for friendships to dissipate his creative energies.

More than anything else he desires to be a doer, but it is only after he gives up every personal dream that he can become strong enough to take the building blocks of his life and put them together. He must literally take the bull by the horns instead of allowing himself to be led through the gossamer Cinderella world his soul remembers.

To accomplish this he would do well to spend much of his time learning self-discipline for only through the ability to guide himself will he ultimately be able to surface from the deep waters in which for lifetimes he has submerged his hopes and his dreams.

The sign which contains the South Node shows the ways in which past-life dreams continue into this incarnation. The sign which contains the North Node indicates how the individual can constructively apply his dreams to reality through expressing creatively all he feels inside.

Some highly evolved souls with these Nodes have experienced Cosmic Consciousness in a former life. Now through their fifth house North Node they are here to bring this awareness to the children of earth.

SIXTH HOUSE NORTH NODE—TWELFTH HOUSE SOUTH NODE

This individual spends most of his time in deep thought. He likes to be left alone so that uninterrupted by others he can let his inner reflections sift through the karmic memories of all his past incarnations. This is not to say that he doesn't like company, or that he's even aware of what he's doing. The fact is that he goes so deep as to become totally oblivious to anything he is thinking about! He loses himself in himself.

Always the conscious reason for going inward is based on logical intention, but the individual tends to reach the point where all logic eludes him. The Neptunian subtlety of the depths he reaches remains a mystery even to him!

One of his greatest problems is that while he stays inside himself he is preventing others from stabilizing his mental journeys. As a result, he accumulates enormous past-life fears, having no idea whether they are real or imagined, or just a compressed collection of the mental scenery on his inward journeys.

Still the basis of his outward life is built on fear and imagination, and regardless of how strong the rest of the chart is, he keeps having moments of not being able to find confidence in himself.

He is a lot like the turtle constantly peeking out of

his shell. People close to him see his life as a tendency to avoid all that seems real.

He spends most of his time watching others from behind a see-through mirror. Ultimately he comes to believe that the rest of the world is viewing him with the same scrutiny. There is a latent paranoia built into this Nodal position.

In areas of work he is an unusually poor organizer, leaving many scattered ends behind him and always feeling that there are not enough hours in the day to complete his chores. His problem is that he doesn't know how to budget his time, and as a result he is constantly trying to catch up to the present.

Much like the rabbit with the clock in *Alice in Wonderland,* he keeps throwing himself into the position of having to rush to avoid being late.

Part of his life will at one time be involved with hospitals, institutions or organizations which demand him to structure his ways. He needs this in order to come out of his inner self.

The big karmic lesson is for him to learn responsibility instead of feeling sorry for all the woes that seem to beset him. More than any other house in the zodiac, he cries at the slightest hurt either real or imagined. Sometimes the crying is inward, but always it is there for on the very deepest levels he feels that the love he has to give goes unnoticed and unappreciated. Because he thinks this way, he becomes his own creator of gloom; and woe to the person who tries to pull him out for then he will have a receptive ear for all the past-life hurts, fears and worries he has not yet even verbalized!

Underneath all else, he is a bottomless well of fretting, with not enough deep faith in the positive outcome of events. He must work on building trust so that he can have the strength to come out of his shell. Once he does, he is one of the most compassionate, beautiful and useful people in the zodiac.

His sixth house North Node gives him great pleasure in helping others, but he cannot do this well until he realizes and accepts the fact that in this incarnation he has chosen a life of sacrfice.

He must learn how to organize his thoughts, his work and his diet, for he is a natural-born healer, capable of defying the limits of practical medicine with his own more mystical methods of curing. But a talent is not a talent until it is developed, and an individual is no more than he thinks he is. Ultimately he will come to learn that his greatest gift is faith. But he will work long and hard to reach that awareness!

Part of the current life will be spent nursing or coping with physical or mental illness, either in himself or others close to him. His major growth occurs when he realizes that all illness is no more than a disharmony in the body reflecting disharmony in thought. Something inside himself is constantly trying to tell him this, and he must learn not to allow his past-life fears to block what is now being opened for him.

Many with these Nodes go through experiences of illnesses that miraculously disappear, to the amazement of medical doctors, dentists and other professional practitioners. The karmic lesson here is to learn the higher reason why, for as soon as understanding is reached, the new-born faith starts to heal. Once he becomes aware of the power of his faith, he becomes a veritable dynamo.

As he builds in more positive thought currents, he automatically learns not to criticize others for the lack of perfection he sees in them.

His outlook on life remains clinical: scrutinizing and diagnosing all he comes in contact with.

Of all the Nodal positions, this is the most difficult one to open up to past incarnations. The twelfth house South Node has completed a karmic path, the details of which are to remain forever sealed in past times, even though the subtle Akashic essence still remains.

Lifetimes of escaping from inner torment have been completed. The individual must come to realize that most of his inner negativity is not related to the current

life, but only exists through his continuing to think along
a track which has already ended.

He still has inner feelings of being persecuted which
he must learn to bury once and for all for the more
he allows himself to dwell in such thoughts, the more
he will inadvertantly recreate such circumstances.

He should learn to realize the past for exactly what
it is: no more than a memory, and no more real than a
photograph in his mind, which he now has the free
choice of holding on to for the sake of its misery or discarding so that he may step out into a productive new
world.

Once he can put his entire state of consciousness
into a positive and productive outlook on life, he will be
able to start experiencing a new meaning to his existence.

The sign which contains the South Node shows the
ways in which the individual blocks his current-life
advancement by withdrawing into karma he has already completed.

The sign which contains the North Node indicates
the ways in which he can now develop a fruitful life
through service.

SEVENTH HOUSE NORTH NODE—FIRST
HOUSE SOUTH NODE

Here the individual has many lessons to learn in
areas of partnerships, marriage and cooperation with
others. In past incarnations he had to account only to
himself for all his thoughts and actions. Now in the
current life, his soul remembers all the individualism
and independence he enjoyed.

While he may pretend to be a good listener for the
sake of society's acceptance, he rarely takes advice
given to him. Instead, he spends most of his energy
developing whatever abilities he has, while constantly
seeking approval for the efforts he has made.

Although he will be the last to admit it openly,
he never quite notices others as much as himself.

He has great apprehensions about being outdone, and will go far out of his way to secure for himself a position where his dominion will not be challenged. If the rest of the horoscope shows strength, then this is truly the individual who wishes to be "King of the Mountain."

Although his experiences in this incarnation teach him to sacrifice for others, he never truly sacrifices himself for he has spent lifetimes building to a point where he has now become an independent spirit.

He can relate to others so long as they don't shackle or bind his sense of freedom. If he feels someone close to him is inhibiting his self-expression he will do all he can to extricate himself from the relationship. Thus, the marriage state is not one that comes easy for him.

Individuals with these Nodes are either single, divorced or at least separated in consciousness from their spouse. They find it difficult to believe that the continuance of their own past-life selfishness is creating all the problems for which they are now blaming others.

They must learn how to give with a whole heart, rather than symbolically throwing a bone here and there just to keep the pack quiet.

This individual is usually so out of harmony with himself as being part of a greater universe that he is prone to develop a chronic impairment or impediment, either physical or emotional, which he ultimately uses for sympathy. The last thing he is willing to accept is a sense of failure, for he constantly feels the need to prove his own self-sufficiency.

Sometimes he is seen by others as a battler, well guarded against any threats to his ego. Since he truly doesn't like to be dependent on others, his loyalties are questionable. Underneath it all his past incarnations have taught him to be faithful to himself, and therein his allegiance ends.

For those who wish to join him he will be their patron, but rarely will he go out of his way to join them. He is a "loner," conscious of his own unique individuality, and proud of the ways in which he knows he can retain it.

His karma is to learn consideration for others, for in his desire to be the center of attention he projects himself as more important than he usually is, thereby shutting out the very love he claims he is being denied. Still, he desires to control others, and in this ability to control he bases his security.

He is capable of great achievements, but he rarely reaches the levels of his capabilities because he is so wrapped up on self that he fails to see the cosmic scope of his personal ideas.

He must learn to view the reflections of his thoughts and actions and to realize that there are always two sides to a coin. Eventually he comes to understand that while both sides of an issue may be totally different, neither is better or worse than the other.

His major growth occurs when he can detach from himself and impersonally laugh at all the ego-centered ideas that ruled him in the past.

He must ultimately come to the point at which he is willing to take all the power, strength and confidence that his prior incarnations have built and give it away to others who need it more. He must do this whole-heartedly without a sense of martyrdom for if his giving becomes ego-involved in any way then he remains on his lonely island. But if his generosity is truly dedicated without pride in giving, then he has an infinite blessing to offer as he inspires confidence and strength in others.

He can give others the will to live where there was none. He can make others aware of their own self-worth. But all the while he is not to ask for anything in return for if he learns to focus his energies on helping others, then he will be amazed to find how God keeps providing all his own needs.

In this Nodal position there is a guaranteed built-in unhappiness every time he focuses his energies on himself. If married he will have much to learn from his second child, as well as in his relationships with nieces and nephews.

He is destined to devote his life to others. Actually he has been preparing for many lifetimes to meet now the person or persons who need him the most. In some cases the spouse is an escapist who must be given the strength and confidence to face reality.

Whether married or single this individual eventually comes to learn that his life is a mission, dedicated to another soul or in fact many souls needing more than he does. His karmic lessons are in developing kindness and an understanding nature. As soon as he does this he is rewarded a thousand to one for all he gives.

The sign which contains the South Node shows the ways in which too much residue. of past-life concern for the self can hamper progress. The sign which contains the North Node shows the ways in which the individual can reach fulfillment through sacrificing the self for others.

EIGHTH HOUSE NORTH NODE—SECOND HOUSE SOUTH NODE

Here the individual is confronted with a powerful battle inside himself on the most basic of levels. His karma is to overcome the extreme possessiveness of his past incarnations. Until he deals with this, he has difficulty finding meaning in anything he cannot personally own. He is jealous of the possessions of others, desiring strongly to have all that his eyes behold. In some individuals this builds up to an insatiable lust for possession. In this respect there is such a strong determination that little can sway him from pursuing his desires.

Nearly always his life is based around the sexual force, and it is nearly certain that the sense of sexual understanding is highly perverted. There is usually someting animalistic about the nature. Whether open or concealed there is a lack of response to the civilizing effects of society.

In his past lives the individual did not fully understand the importance of other people's values but continued to go his own way, unaware of how he affected others. His soul has built a need system so great that no matter how much he is fulfilled, his greatest needs always seem to be just beyond his reach. He is like the proverbial donkey following a carrot strapped to his head, but rarely does he understand that he is the one who put it there.

Those near him would give him the Moon if it would make him happy, but they know as well as he does that it would be only a momentary toy ultimately to be discarded and replaced by another need. It seems to be the quantity of quality that he desires, which is to say that he feels he must have all! A bundle of excess in all directions, he finds it difficult to change his ways even after the realization that he is headed down a path of disaster. He pushes each crossroad to such extreme excess that when he does discover his errors, he is so far beyond the point of departure that he finds it impossible to see his way back. And so he continues further along a path he knows is wrong because it is the only road his eyes can see.

In some cases he goes to such extremes that he may run into trouble with the law, but long after he sees his error he still keeps trying to convince others that he is right.

More than one with any other Nodal position this individual must learn self-control for without discipline he can too easily allow his past incarnation habits of self-indulgence to make a shambles of his current life.

Some with these Nodes experience an infirmity which brings them so close to death that their eyes open to a new appreciation of life. Others go through extremely trying sexual episodes so that they may start to be more clinical about their behavior. But always the karmic lesson is the same. The individual pushes himself so hard that he ulimately destroys all ground he has gained. Through a symbolic death of excessive behavior patterns he may ultimately experience a new birth.

The past life residue presents too many physical and material concerns. The main growth in the current life is based on the indivudal's ability to ferret from out of the depths of his being the strength for a rebirth. He often displays an interest in the occult through which he ultimately gains information needed to achieve his regenerative transformation.

Whatever he chooses to do there is always chaos in it for he is an extremist. And yet the combined karmic residue of stubborness and laziness keeps stalling his rebirth. His soul wants to transform, but he has difficulty finding enough energy to do it.

The hardest thing for him is to learn how to walk with no footsteps for he so desperately wants to be impressive that he keeps making his own life heavier.

Relationships are extremely important to him. From prior incarnations he has developed the habit of seeing the world as a social caste system and within this framework keeps struggling for status, always believing that some people are more privileged than others. Through his eighth house North Node he must symbolically kill this past-life value system and go through the permanent metamorphosis which will eventually attune him to the value of others. He has much to learn from those close to him as soon as he starts to listen.

Most of his sexual thoughts come from a deep-seated desire to kill the physical plane. They lead him on a path of ultimate disgust with himself as well as with the physical and material life he has led for so long. Through open or secret lust as well as jealousies in money or business affairs he keeps spiraling his life to a point of no return. Once he reaches this, he will begin to be accepted through other people's value systems in order to find his way back. But he will be confronted with the test of having to give up all that he has ever thought important, almost as if he is being asked to step to the back of the line and wait his turn. Each time a new and finer value is imposed on him, he must learn how to eliminate all in himself that blocks its acceptance.

He will start his new life from the bottom of the ladder, where because of the slowness of his ascent he will treasure deeply every inch of ground he gains.

Truly these Nodes indicate a difficult life, but only because the ingrained attitudes of past incarnations are so fixed on having their own way.

Until the transition is complete he can expect his current life to be one financial tug of war after another. He must learn the karmic lesson that possessions are for the purpose of *use* and that it is not necessary to own more than what is immediately useful.

When he overcomes the tendency to allow his life's energies to dissipate themselves, he can become a veritable dynamo in the business world. Still he must never forget that he is the type that must burn his bridges behind him as a protection against slipping backward to levels he has struggled to pass through.

He must understand the biblical story of Lot, who when he was finally redeemed from Sodom and Gomorrha was asked to leave the city, take no possessions and under no circumstances look back.

The eighth house North Node can regenerate or degenerate the individual. It is up to the strength of his own faith. To reach heaven this Nodal position must walk through hell first, and there from the very bowels of the earth make the realization that God will hear his faintest cry for help as soon as he sincerely promises not to "look back."

The sign which contains the South Node shows the type of past-life value system that must be regenerated. The sign which contains the North Node shows the ways in which the rebirth will be accomplished.

NINTH HOUSE NORTH NODE—THIRD HOUSE
SOUTH NODE   RC ♋ ♐

This individual is forever pulling himself out of webs of entanglement. Every relationship he enters becomes so complicated that he has to use all his energies to free himself. In past incarnations he developed a great need for people, and herein lies his weak spot for as much as he now thinks he would like to be alone he feels an almost compelling need to reach for others.

He listens to problems and likes to be in the position of giving advice. Often frustrated by the multitude of problems dumped in his lap, he secretly thinks that if he had had more education he would be better equipped to cope with all the questions that befall him. He keeps trying to be as diplomatic as possible and is constantly enmeshed in the after-thoughts of the words he has spoken to others.

Always conscious of the interpretation his words may be given, he nurtures an inner fear of being misunderstood. As a result he keeps going back to yesterday's conversation to re-explain all that he meant.

He must understand the essence of truth without having to feel compelled to make truth smaller by trying to communicate it verbally to others.

One of his greatest problems is dealing with the karmic residue of an insatiable curiosity, which although it served him well in former incarnations now keeps leading him deeper into webs of details. His greatest crises occur each time he is forced to make decisions for rather than relying on his intuition or his higher mind, he keeps seeking more facts and details in the hope that when he has all the information the decision making process will be easier.

Constantly striving to achieve neutrality he becomes a paradox to himself. In prior lives he fell into the habit of identifying with catchy phrases, cute sayings and euphemisms to the point that he has now become a walking cliche.

Liking to read and explore a wonderland of knowledge that he sees around him, his life is a constant thirst for more understanding. He is convinced that this is the one path in life that has no end. Whatever he becomes keenly interested in he can make into a life-long study, particularly if the South Node is in a fixed sign.

He likes to feel worldly. As a result he'll do things that others wouldn't just for the sake of experiencing new understanding.

His current life is involved with so many people that hurt feelings are bound to fly, not because of any malicious intent but rather through the inability to keep up with everyone in whose life he has become involved. At the very deepest of levels he has many inner doubts about himself which become amplified when he speaks with others, for if it were at all possible he would try to be all things to all people.

As a result of past-life habits, he spends too much time in "lower mind." He goes through more movement than he has to, and if this is not expressed physically, then he does it in thought. At times his merry-go round of possibilities is so great that he thoroughly drains himself by thinking about what he should do. As a result he does nothing.

He will experience fears that he is sexually impotent. Once he starts questioning along this track his enormous thirst for understanding can lead him into a promiscuous behavior pattern until he is reassured that all is well and he is perfectly normal.

On his deepest level he is not a sexual animal but in fact so mentally inclined that he has fears of being shut out from the nitty-gritty of life because of his mental inclinations.

Like the young child afraid his peers will accuse him of being a bookworm, he will dare himself to prove that he can be accepted in a physically-oriented world. Nevertheless, his greatest subconscious need is one day to become a walking encyclopedia so that he will never be caught short, lacking the right piece of information at the right moment.

His biggest growth comes when he learns how to make the karmic transition from lower to higher mind. As he drops his past-life attachment to trivia, his eyes begin to open wide to the enormous horizons before him.

The less he talks to others the more faith he starts to develop.

He must learn how constantly to broaden his interests so that his scope of knowledge is not limited by the demands of his immediate circle of relationships. He does well when he learns how to step back so that he can see the forest from the trees. When he does this he also learns how to let things slide off his back, which gives him a new sense of peace that somehow always eluded his reach.

Traveling helps to broaden his perspective, and he meets his greatest successes far from his place of birth. For some the life will be influenced greatly by a foreigner.

Through the ninth house North Node, enormous spiritual growth is possible once the individual has learned how to pull away from all his prior-life doubts and questions. He must take his mind out of a finite world and focus on an infinite consciousness.

He will lose friends by doing this for there are few who will fully understand his sudden aloofness. But through those who stay with him he will learn the difference between a friend and an acquaintance. As he grows he begins to focus on ideas rather than the words through which the ideas are expressed. He sees how others limit themselves by language and tries to speak to their ideas rather than to their words. The sign which contains the South Node indicates the ways in which the soul memory of past incarnations is still too embedded in lower mind activities. The sign which contains the North Node shows the ways in which the individual can now free himself through the broadening influence of his higher mind.

TENTH HOUSE NORTH NODE—FOURTH HOUSE SOUTH NODE

Here the individual finds that much of his time is needed for the demands of his family. Constantly he feels held down, as if he is being prevented from realizing his own individuality. The fact is that he comes into the current life with much karma owed to his family.

In past incarnations he ignored the hands that fed him. Now he is locked into the lesson of becoming those feeding hands himself. In the current life he finds his mate and children just as highly unappreciative of all he tries to do for them. Still he will do more if he is ever to grow past his karma. At times the burdens become so heavy that he has to fight himself to keep from feeling an inner resentment.

The female with these Nodes will have problems with at least one child which will demand most of her time, effort, energy and concern for she is to learn on the very deepest of levels the responsibilities of parenthood. To enforce the karma still deeper, the spouse is either not present or so lacking in character that this indiviual must ultimately become mother and father at the same time.

Whether positive or negative the emotions never leave the family. This individual constantly feels the need to break out and be free; yet his past-life memories of self-enforced chains never quite permit him to do this.

Nearly all of his energy is spent on untangling the web of relations that he sees around him.

In some instances, he experiences great conflict with other family members over real estate

He must learn not to let circumstances weigh him down with feelings of hopelessness, for the needs of his family are constantly compounding themselves, to the point that from time to time they become considerably more than he bargained for.

Often, he is caught by surprise through the actions of those closest to him for although he can develop a

strong outer worldliness, he still remains amost childishly naive when it comes to the emotions he feels
about those close to him.

Some with these Nodes have to go out to work, becoming the sole source of family support. Others are
put into the position of becoming the family supervisor.

Always this individual is caught between the conflict of the things he would like to do for himself and
the things he knows he must do for his loved ones.

Constantly faced with situations which tempt him
to react childishly, he must learn how to mature. He
must rise above family disharmony and do all he can
to achieve a role of self-dignity.

When the needs of his loved ones are understood,
only then can he have the freedom to experience a
career life of his own.

As he makes the switch to his tenth house North
Node, he is ultimately forced into the position of assuming the dominant role. He must learn how to keep
his life focused in a direction above and beyond all the
scattering needs of his close family members.

Paradoxically, he escapes from one family by creating another, until ultimately every person he meets
and likes gets pulled closer to him in a type of pseudo-
universal family. As the years build up the life starts
to resemble the "old woman who lived in a shoe."

His greatest happiness comes from being in a position to be able to offer shelter to others.

In later years he joyously re-invites others to lean
on him. His mission to move away from emotional
immaturity and in the direction of responsibility tells
him that each person he moves along the path represents another payment for his own ticket towards soul
evolution.

The sign which contains the South Node shows the
ways in which he allows immaturity on the part of
others as well as himself to block his potentialities
for achievement. The sign which contains the North
Node indicates the ways in which he can develop maturity by pointing his life in a meaningful direction.

*ELEVENTH HOUSE NORTH NODE—FIFTH
HOUSE SOUTH NODE*

Here the individual comes into the current life re-
membering a style of living in which he was the sole
creator. Now he keeps trying to take the bull by the
horns in order to recreate the manner of living to which
he was accustomed. Yet everything he tries to do bears
a tinge of being slightly inappropriate insofar as fitting
his current life circumstances.

He is prone to love affairs, finding them a comfort
to the continuation of his past-life ego. What he often
fails to realize is that through his love affairs he makes
himself weaker, and rather than gaining strength from
compliments and encouragements he develops a dependency where each compliment creates the need for
another. Eventually he makes himself so helpless that
his behavior becomes hopelessly childlike.

He wants to be loved desperately, but the residue
of past-life sexual tensions are so great that he often
confuses what is really important to him. He has great
difficulty understanding reality for his life is stage
of players and his dreams are so romantic in nature
that he becomes a veritable Don Quixote chasing windmills. He believes in chivalry and can easily be fooled
by glamor. Wanting to be constantly reassured that his
arrival in life does not go unnoticed, he is unable to
accept the role of just being a member of the audience.

To those who appreciate him he can be extremely
generous, but the moment he feels ignored he will run
into his gossamer dream world trying to create a
Seventeenth Century romantic adventure in which he
will be the central character.

Constantly in search of self-fulfillment through am-
orous adventures, he can too easily lose his way.

He would like others to think of him as sacrificial
and when he does involve himself with a love affair it
is almost certain that he will force himself into a position of having to give up everything. Like the "Martyr
King" who sacrificed his throne so that he might fulfill

his love, this individual would like his affairs to be honored, sanctioned and even admired.

His past-life sense of dignity is so great that he is not particularly pleased with even the thought of an illicit love affair; yet from time to time he finds himself in the midst of one if for no other reason than to express his ability to sacrifice a principle for what he believes at the moment to be the world's greatest love.

Basically he is a good person and it would take severe chart afflictions for him to have a malicious bone in his body. Throughout all the zodiac his creative talents with children are unsurpassed, for at heart he is a child himself.

Regardless of his Sun sign he will at one time in this life need to lean on someone with more strength than himself.

Through his eleventh house North Node he is to learn the value of friendship. He must transcend the physically possessive relationships of his past incarnations and cherish with equal fervor the new impersonal relationships he is now forming.

In this life he is learning how to pay more attention to the meaning of his dreams rather than trying to force his own will against the flowing tide.

His dreams bring him messages from his higher guidance through which he is telepathically brought to understand the reasons for all his actions, but his will is often so great that he refuses to accept what he knows is true.

If he is realistically asked to abdicate anything at all in this life, it would only be his powerful self-will for here in the pride of ego he actually blocks all that he so desperately desires. Truly, he is his own worst enemy.

The individual with these Nodes suffers from a built-in discontent for whatever he creates through his South Node only leaves him free to dream of more he is missing. He would like to be free of entanglements, but he is constantly jumping out of the frying pan into the fire. Before any growth at all can be made he must learn to overcome the monstrous dragon ego which he has allowed to become his self-generating instrument of destruction. He must learn how to see himself impersonally, with the understanding that his life is like a river flowing beneath the bridge from whose vantage point he may watch it.

His most difficult tests always revolve around the temptation to control the flow of that river, yet his greatest happiness occurs when he can appreciate its beauty without tampering.

It is almost certain that he will go through at least one major experience in which he will be required to sacrifice his personal ego for the sake of fairness to another; for only when he has learned how to rid himself of every biased thought can he reach his higher purpose. So long as he retains the slightest tinge of self-pride all the power in his chart will be denied him. Even the possibilities of a harmonious marriage loom beyond his reach until he becomes impersonal.

The fifth house South Node uses so much energy in trying to achieve self-sympathy that the individual has difficulty finding the strength to give complete fulfillment to a marriage mate. Many with these Nodes experience divorce, but this is neither destiny nor necessity. It is simply an outgrowth of misusing the South Node energies. Through so much focusing on the self the individual does not see or fully appreciate all the blessings he has. Again the answer is the same. He must relinquish the grip on "self" and dedicate his life to impersonal service rather than expect others to wait on him.

If he can learn to become less romantic and more scientific, he will start to see truth for what it is. He must never allow the fires of passion to cloud his vision for his happiness will be achieved only when he can look at life from a dispassionate viewpoint.

His karma is in learning how to become non-involved and yet always available when needed by others.

Ultimately, he is destined to become the impersonal servant of humanity.

He will at one time in this life do much to further the career of another.

Friendships, clubs and societies become important to him for it is through such associations with others that he ultimately comes to sense his own identity. Through the ways that others value him he comes to value himself. Then he is able to see himself as a part of others as well as a part of a higher cause to which he is dedicated.

The more he can do this the more he will rise off the plane of self-consciousness, and the demanding needs to gratify his own ego will become submerged in the collective ego of the cause to which he has dedicated his identity.

When he completes this lesson, his strength of character and sense of direction become no weaker nor less purposeful than the cause of which he becomes a part.

The sign which contains the South Node shows the ways in which this individual allows too much past-life residue of passion and desire to pressure his current life. The sign which contains the North Node indicates the ways in which he can develop enough detachment so that he frees his personal self, enabling him to dedicate his energies toward more universal causes.

TWELFTH HOUSE NORTH NODE—SIXTH HOUSE SOUTH NODE

Here the individual undergoes a crisis in consciousness. Whether he is actually aware of it or not, much of his life is spent in deep thought.

He finds the physical world exhausting. From time to time he has to deal with illnesses which take him out of the competitive arena, strongly afflicting his abilities to work.

When he is working he finds conditions intolerable. He feels either underpaid or at the very least unappreciated for all he has to offer. He becomes so wrapped up in the circumstances surrounding whatever he is doing that he allows his attitudes toward his job to permeate all areas of his life.

He has much prior-life memories of order and organization, yet everywhere he goes he sees chaos.

In past incarnations he was a perfectionist, critical of the world around him. Now the imperfections he sees weaken him to the point that he feels unable to cope. The world is perceived as not quite giving him all that it could.

Some with these Nodes tend to dwell in self-pity, while others nourish an embittered resentment. There are feelings of jealousy directed toward other people's well-being, which they perceive as being less earned than their own. Usually there is an inflated sense of ego at the source of the problem. The self as developed in past incarnations is now seen as a perfected ideal, stationed above the rest of humanity.

In his own private thoughts this individual will rarely admit that he has a tendency to look down upon others. Yet, secretly he sees everyone as less perfect than himself.

He would sooner go unemployed than work at a job which he feels is beneath him. It is certain, however, that circumstances will force him to do such work even though it is against his every principle.

Having tendencies to internalize his anger at feeling put down he creates one very real illness after another, until ultimately he reaches the point that he feels justified in blaming his work conditions for his poor state of health.

Carrying a past incarnation feeling that society has shut him out, he sees himself as a neglected child deprived of the central core of richness in life which is there for others but somehow not for himself. He spends too much energy trying to impress others and not enough in developing a fullness within himself. More than anything else he must learn to look inside, where he will find the answers to all of his problems.

Many with these Nodes watch life pass them by, spending all too much of their time and energy wrapped up in petty thoughts. There is a strong residue of past-life nervousness in the sixth house South Node wherein this individual literally eats away at himself by trying to digest into his system of order every tiny detail that comes to his attention.

He must learn how to discriminate between what is important in terms of his life's values and what are just transitory upsets which will pass in due time.

Through his constant questioning he creates for himself a sexual problem, rooting itself deeply in fears of failure. And so unable is he to face his fears that he will compound the problem by developing a pattern of abnormal sexual response designed to mask his feelings of inadequacy.

Though he tries not to, he keeps seeing himself as a helpless pebble on a beach of thousands. In prior lives he managed to control his universe. Now the world seems larger than he would like and he does all he can to prevent himself from feeling too small by comparison.

His growth starts the moment he begins to see himself not only as part of a greater whole but containing within himself the essence of the entire universe. He must break his past incarnation tendency to put the world in little boxes and search for the seed of all within himself. Here he will find the abundant richness he has been so desperately seeking.

Periods of forced isolation help to bring him to a higher consciousness through which he ultimately learns that things can be different without one necessarily being better or worse than the other.

By going deep into himself he will realize that all of life's conditions depend entirely on how much he can relinquish his hold on trying to overturn the world and rechannel his energies toward overturning himself.

He does well by immersing himself in the works of a large institution where he can develop a group-consciousness, focusing on the collective good of the whole rather than dwelling in the collected residue of his past-life bitterness.

He will be tested many times in areas which help him to develop compassion, until he ultimately sees that judging others actually prevents his own happiness.

His past-life karma is erased when he learns how to flow rather than allow his life to keep interrupting itself by petty distractions. He must attune himself to the essence of the universe rather than attempt to sort everything into neat little compartments. The compartments are like a house of cards, and only after they topple does he start to realize that his purpose in life is very far from what he originally thought.

He can then learn how to loosen up and bathe in the beauty of all God's creation, rather than seeing only a part of God and calling the part he sees All. As soon as he can greet change willingly, bending while the winds of circumstance flow through his being, he is on the path.

Eventually he will leave the world where people manipulate each other and walk through the doorway to a higher harmony. In preparation, he must transcend the subconscious past-life memories of physical problems that still weigh him down and start to climb the cosmic ladder which leads to the realization of his soul. He must learn how to appreciate the wonder of all he sees without enmeshing himself in the details of why or how.

His life will represent the ending of an idea much as the works of Dante symbolized the end of a period in literature. When he accepts this, his life's work can be a great culmination of all that has come before him.

Although his work may bring him behind the scenes there is a good possibility that it can come to public attention. He must also learn that the physical state of his health is totally dependent upon the purity and stability of his inner mind.

Truly this is the Nodal position of mind over matter, and the life will be a karmic transition from the world of matter into the consciousness of infinite spirit.

The sign which contains the South Node indicates the ways in which former incarnations brought the individual to preoccupy himself with physical matter. The sign which contains the North Node shows how he can now transform his soul into the pure essence of Divine Mind.

CHAPTER FIVE

ASPECTS TO THE NODES

The desirability of one Node over the other is not a constant. Until such time as the South Node has performed at its highest possible level, the individual will find less reward in the North Node than he expects.

Since the South Node symbolizes a culmination of behavioral characteristics from many lifetimes, it would only be by bringing such behavior through a progressive evolution that the individual would be ready to benefit from his North Node.

If he puts the cart before the horse, he is too liable to approach his North Node in its most negative sense; but if he strives to overcome the ways in which his South Node is holding him back, then he will find Divine Guidance in the surprise blessings his North Node yields.

CONJUNCTIONS TO THE SOUTH NODE

Karmic lessons, taking more than one lifetime to learn, show up with strong planetary conjunctions to the South Node. The addition of such planetary energies to the soul's remembrance of its purpose creates a mandatory condition wherein the South Node lessons are to be lived again.

This configuration should not necessarily be deemed a negative condition. Individuals who have acquired a great deal of knowledge or talent are thusly afforded

a second chance at bringing their accomplishments to
a flowering culmination.

CONJUNCTIONS TO THE NORTH NODE

Planetary conjunctions to the North Node urge the
individual to leave his past behind. Instead, he will
experience a new karmic lesson in the current life.
During his younger years, he tends to misuse his
North Node until he is able to discover its latent potential.

Occasionally, he tries to fall back on his South Node,
but each time he does he finds circumstances which
are so unbearably intolerable that he again chooses to
re-evaluate his North Node possibilities. Ultimately he
realizes that he is being subliminally pressured to step
forward into a uniquely new experience.

MUTUAL RECEPTION

When the ruling planet of either Node is in the sign
of the opposite Node, then the matter of mutual reception is to be considered.

Here, the past and present are so unavoidably
linked that it will be necessary for the individual to
draw on his past in order to fulfill his present. He
does not have to repeat the past unless planet conjunctions to the South Node create pressure for him to do so.
Nevertheless, he will be given strong glimpses of it
so that he will remember how to stumble upon the information he needs to meet his future.

CONJUNCTIONS TO BOTH NODES

When planets conjunct both Nodes, the soul is confronted with the resolution of a very powerful conflict
which may not be postponed beyond the present life.

If the individual is able to focus on the energies of
the less detrimental or more benefic planet, then he
can build enough strength gradually to overcome his

susceptibilities to the negative energies of the more detrimental planet. By so doing, he can evolve his soul to the point that he will ultimately reap benefit from even the most malefic of configurations.

If a planet near either Node seems to be holding him back, he must learn how to attune himself to receive and then express the more refined and absolutely subtle higher frequencies of that planet.

SQUARES TO THE NODES

Planets which square both Nodes act as distractions to the central theme in life. They represent areas in which the individual in past incarnations has allowed himself to scatter off his path. Now he finds these planets as detours on his road home.

The more squares there are to the nodes, the more the individual experiences agonizing frustrations which seem to block him from his purpose. If the squares are powerful enough, he may spend so much energy in trying to settle them that he may delude himself into believing that his squares rather than his Nodes represent his largest direction. He will be guided to lessons of sacrifice in addition to his specific karma.

TRINES TO THE SOUTH NODE

Planets which trine the South Node afford the individual with opportunities symbolically to relive and improve upon his past. The conditions through which he can do this are usually external to the self, even though their ultimate effect on the self is to build it within.

There is a necessity to guard against dissipation, particularly if the South Node is in a mutable or water sign. In some cases, the individual must learn self-respect, for the easy trines make it almost too inviting for him to sneak out of life through the back door.

TRINES TO THE NORTH NODE

Planets which trine the North Node hold the promise of a richly-rewarding life experience. External life opportunities will be harmonious with the direction in which the soul is moving. Thus, the individual may find himself advancing in life while he is advancing smoothly in karma at the same time.

Naturally, this assumes that planetary energies are not grossly misused to the point that benefics act like malefics and malefics become symbolic of "hell" itself!

Nevertheless, not only will the North Node experience be easier to reach, but the individual also will find his path aided by outside encouragement.

CHAPTER SIX

CHART DELINEATIONS

The chart delineations in this chapter have been selected in order to present the student with the Gestalt method of chart interpretation.

The full horoscope including the Nodes represents a symbolic picture of the total soul as viewed through its present incarnation. Thus, any and all inharmonious factors within the chart are still harmoniously integrated within the singular soul entity under consideration.

Complete understanding of the horoscope is much like the threading of a needle. The loose fibers at the end of the thread go in all different directions, but they are part of the original thread. Still the needle cannot be threaded until all these loose fibers are wound together. When the thread is brought to a single point, it fits through the eye of the needle easily.

In like manner, the Nodes must always agree with the rest of the horoscope. Each planetary configuration is as a brush stroke to a painting, but together the painting is more than just a summation of brush strokes.

Through careful study of the full horoscope, it becomes possible to pull all the loose thread fibers and sundry brush strokes together so that the singular reason for life can emerge.

Charts read in this way are interpreted on the soul level, and thus have infinitely more meaning for the individual, who after all is much more than his personality desires, transitory illnesses, and emotional frustrations.

✦ *EDGAR CAYCE*

Here we find the Pisces-Virgo Nodes with the North Node in the 7th house conjunct Saturn. This conjunction is our first indication that the karma and the mission are harmonious with each other.

The 1st house South Node indicates that in this incarnation the soul is not here for itself, but rather for the purpose of dedicating the life through sacrifice (Pisces) to others (7th house). This is confirmed further by so much of the chart's weight in the western hemisphere.

Pisces is the sign of cosmic consciousness while Virgo is the sign of finite consciousness. The life work here would be to teach (Saturn conjunct Mercury) the existence of something more (North Node in Pisces) than the purely mechanical nature (South Node in Virgo) through which man looks at himself (1st house).

To accomplish this, four Pisces planets accompany the North Node, giving the chart a broader perspective of universal understanding. To be able to attune to the more subtle psychic vibrations Cayce would have to be a gentle man, and this is aided by the Pisces Venus.

In beginner texts of mundane astrology a Pisces Mercury is designated as poorly placed with an inability to crystallize thought. When used on higher planes, however, as Cayce unquestionably did, it allows for an unlimited flow of ideas as well as cosmic messages. Saturn conjunct the Mercury shows that these ideas were to be put to some practical use for humanity.

With three planets in Taurus, Cayce was very much a Venus-Neptune soul, which accounts so much for his willingness to throw his life on the altar of sacrifice so that civilization could make one more step toward understanding what was thought to be beyond understanding.

Pluto, the planet which rules the unknown as well as mass thinking, is placed in his career house conjunct the Moon. This conjunction is always the sign of a direct psychic. In addition, the already-sensitized

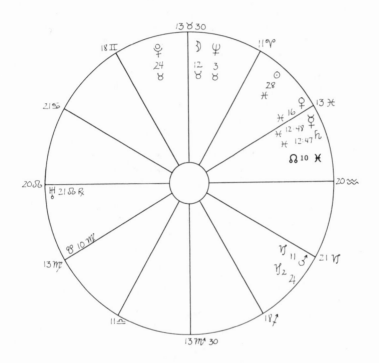

EDGAR CAYCE

3—18—1877

HOPKINSVILLE, KENTUCKY

Taurus Moon is conjunct Neptune which still further increases its receptivity. These three planets in Taurus would make Cayce so attuned to other world forces that he would at times find normal life difficult.

The interesting thing is that whenever we speak of Pisces, the message is *not* the message. Much of the world today that is interested in psychic phenomena and spiritual growth looks to Cayce as a pacesetter and an example to follow. And yet they are following the wrong message.

Because his work was so profound and seemingly miraculous, people tend to follow the miracles instead of the message behind the miracles. Jesus performed miracles only to whet people's appetites for the kingdom of heaven.

Spiritual leaders ever since have been given powers to perform in order to attract the otherwise apathetic ears of the world to a higher music. With Saturn-Mercury and the North Node in the 7th house in Pisces, Cayce was here to teach a lesson in marriage. He lived for his marriage and considered it to be the most important thing in his life, far beyond any miracles he may have participated in. He shines as an example that no man is greater than his ability to humble himself to another. The further implication is that marriage is NEVER an impediment to spiritual growth or pscyhic development. All of his work with karma was to teach people the value of Universal Love (Venus in Pisces in the 8th house of other people's values).

This message was so important for mankind that Cayce was also given Uranus in Leo in the 1st house so that his impact would be extremely powerful. And yet, he never used power for the sake of power. Through his 1st house South Node he was aware of the destructive impulses stimulated by the ego, and he taught that man's ego keeps on creating and recreating the karma he brings upon himself.

Whenever we are dealing with an evolved soul, the Virgo South Node represents prior life purification. In addition, with so many of his planets above the horizon, particularly the 9th house Moon, much of his own personal karma was already taken care of before this incarnation.

Perhaps the only negative thing in the entire chart would be the Mars-Jupiter conjunction in the 5th house, which at times pushed him a bit too hard (Capricorn). And yet, this was necessary for him to create a work so monumental that the Piscean subtlety of his message would be eventually realized.

Through his 8th house Pisces Sun, he was to impart to mankind a legacy of understanding so that one day man would come to know that all his suffering is the direct result of his own causes.

ROBERT REDFORD

Here we find the Sagittarius North Node in the fifth house of acting and creative talent. In the case of a movie star we always note how the motion pictures that they are magnetized to do symbolically express the chart energies. In "Downhill Racer," Redford played the part of an Olympic Ski Champion, thus combining the great outdoors of his Sagittarian North Node with the Mars competitiveness (Mars conjunct the North Node) which ultimately won him the Gold Medal. Sagittarius is also the sign of gambling, which was the basic theme of "The Sting." In "Jeremiah Johnson," Redford played the part of an outdoors-man, again re-iterating the Sagittarian theme.

The eleventh house South Node in Gemini indicates prior lifetimes of dreaming and wishing to sample all the different and varied interests in life. He would come into this incarnation with a developed curiosity about knowledge of all types. This, coupled with his Sagittarius North Node conjunct Mars would now give him an intense thirst for life.

With all the fire trinity well represented, he is able to exude an enthusiastic outlook which sparks others; and while his Aries Midheaven gives him strong appeal

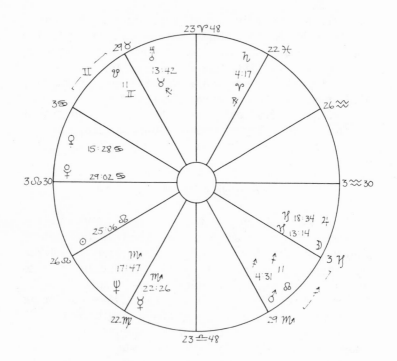

ROBERT REDFORD

8—18—1937

SANTA MONICA, CALIF.

to young audiences, his Capricorn Moon gives him equal strength with older people. Thus, the scope of his magnetism is enormously wide.

This is one of those very rare horoscopes which contain a triple Grand Trine. The first house Sun in Leo, the fifth house North Node, the Aries Midheaven and Uranus in the tenth give Redford the kind of life in which the world can literally be his oyster.

But if the chart is viewed in terms of all the lucky aspects it contains, the point of Redford's life would be missed.

The Sagittarius-Gemini Nodes always indicate an incarnation of a Messenger. And with the Sagittarius North Node in the Aries decanate of the sign, a mutual reception is formed with his 9th house Saturn. This brings the karma, the message and the mission into the realm of higher mind.

Redford's present incarnation is timed in accordance with this higher message. He reached enormous success in 1974 when his Nodes were crossed by the transiting Nodes, just at the time when "The Sting" became the most talked-about picture of the year. All this occurred while Saturn transited his 12th house, indicating that this success was karmically due him.

Since the days of Joe Dimaggio, America has been lacking heroes with whom to identify. As a result, the country has experienced an inability to identify with success. Redford's mission is to help restore faith in the individual (Aries Saturn in the 9th house). And in any ways he chooses to do this (5th house North Node in Sagittarius), the universe will cooperate with him. Moreover, the more flamboyant his approach (Leo rising, Sun in the 1st house), the better, since his karmic mission is to show the world how to win!

In each of his pictures he portrays the role of intense seriousness toward the accomplishment of a personal goal (Capricorn Moon square Aries Saturn). Always there are insurmountable odds which he miraculously overcomes. His attitude is that he never expected to lose.

It's no accident that Redford's career reached the top while the rest of the world was in the depths of depression. He stands as a symbol of man's ability to override the negative conditions of the world he lives in and reach the potential he was born with!

CHRISTINE JORGENSON

In the chart of Christine Jorgenson we find the Cancer-Capricorn Nodes, which are always indicative of a shift in the hormonal balance. The Capricorn South Node in the 4th house would show Christine's early years in this life to be more influenced by trying to continue prior life patterns of masculine dominance. As Capricorn indicates the father role, there would be much soul memory of living up to masculine expectations. As maturity sets in, an individual tends to lean more to their 10th house than their 4th, and in doing so Christine would be confronted with the Cancer North Node, which is so peculiarly feminine by contrast. The Moon-ruled Cancer allows for the free flowing of the female emotion, whereas the Capricorn South Node has a tendency to block the normal emotional flow.

With both Nodes in Cardinal signs, new beginnings here are indicated. As Capricorn is a sign of bringing things to a conclusion (it rules the gates of death through which the soul leaves the body), and as Cancer has rulership over birth, we can see that this soul in the current incarnation is completing one way of life in order that it may start on a new path. Pluto forming a conjunction with the North Node shows this to be a total transformation and is the first indicator that it would be of a sexual nature. The North Node itself is in the Scorpio decanate of Cancer, which again points to sexuality as the vehicle of the regeneration.

The mission in life as indicated by Saturn also falls in Scorpio, but here it is symbolic of even more than sexual transformation. With Saturn placed in the 3rd house and Pluto in the 10th, this change not only would be monumental, but the full impact of it would have

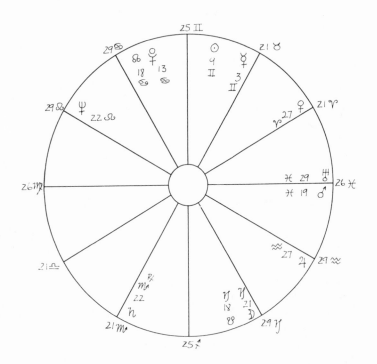

CHRISTINE JORGENSON

5—30—1926

NEW YORK, NEW YORK

to be communicated to the masses. Interestingly, Saturn is in the Cancer decanate of Scorpio while Pluto and the North Node are in the Scorpio part of Cancer—a kind of mutual reception showing that all three are indeed working together.

The remainder of the chart shows how the soul would bring about this change, as well as how society would react to it, The Moon-Pluto opposition indicates that the change would not only be public in nature, but also that it would stir great controversy. Many people have had sex-change operations, but only Christine Jorgenson was designated as the messenger, making known to a confused society that such a change was not only possible but also desirable and compatible for all those suffering with similar feelings.

To bring this about, Christine's soul chose to be born as a Gemini with a 9th house Sun and Mercury in its ruling sign. It is important to realize here that while Gemini was the necessary Sun sign to communicate the idea, if it had not been posited in the 9th house (of independent thought and attitudes), the Gemini tendency to be swayed by others might well have been strong enough to prevent such an untraditional operation completely.

The Mars-Uranus conjunction is also indicative of sexual changes. As Mars (sex) falls in the 6th house, which is so often characteristic of operations, it shows that sexuality would play a large part in the health picture. At the same time, Uranus in the 7th house shows that Christine would have to change completely her ideas concerning marriage mates. Here also we find sexuality stressed, as Uranus falls in the Scorpio decanate of Pisces.

Jupiter in Aquarius trine the Midheaven indicates good fortune in experiencing that which is new and different and uniquely ahead of its time. As Jupiter is the planet which brings us our truth and Aquarius is the sign which is always highly individualistic, Christine would have to go far from the norms of society to reach her own higher wisdom.

Her Aries Venus in the 8th house shows new beginnings in areas of love and sex as well as specifically indicating a fresh start in experiencing the feminine principle.

The Capricorn Moon which is so peculiarly sensitive to even the slightest negative vibration becomes a powerful regenerative force here as it helps complete the T square of Venus to both Nodes. Very deep inner emotional reactions in childhood would cause so much discomfort that Christine would be forced to make a fresh start through the point of the T square, which falls in the 8th house (sexual rebirth).

There was further incentive to do this through the Neptune-Venus trine from the 11th house to the 8th, which would have prompted dreams of what it would feel like to be a woman.

We can see that the entire chart cooperates with the Nodes so that the Soul can have the incentives and opportunities to work out its karma.

MARTIN LUTHER KING

In the chart of Martin Luther King we find the Taurus-Scorpio Nodes. Here the soul karma is to move away from the past of Scorpio's violence into the peace of Venus-ruled Taurus. The 7th house South Node indicates that in former incarnations this soul would have suffered through the destructive impulses of others. In this life, there was an identification to be made with building the self (first house Taurus) in a substantial but non-violent way.

Through his life, however, there were always those who set themselves up as his advisors (partners so to speak) who constantly reflected his South Node back to him. In other words, non-violent peace marches would keep turning into Scorpionic melees as a result of the ideas of others.

The 7th house which also represents open adversaries falls in Scorpio, which is anything but an open

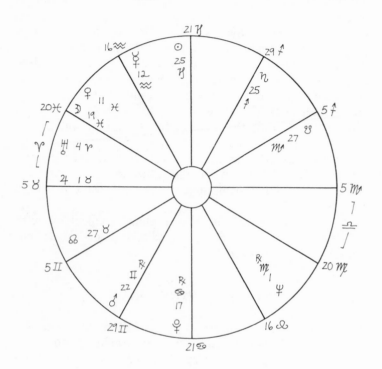

MARTIN LUTHER KING

1—15—1929

ATLANTA, GEORGIA

sign. Thus, with his South Node here and two planets in his 12th house, King had many hidden enemies. This was not so much because they disagreed with what he was trying to do, since he did stand for a Universal Cosmic Principle, but more with his techniques of bringing it about. The Taurus North Node has all the patience in the world and is willing to work toward something slowly, while the Scorpio South Node wants revolution yesterday.

Interestingly enough, his Nodes fall in the two signs which were the Sun and Moon signs of Gautama Buddha, whose life represented very similar principles. When we see strong similarities between different charts it almost suggests that the different souls may have received part of their teaching in the same place.

In the case of Martin Luther King, his Saturn mission in the 8th house was to leave a legacy of hope (Sagittarius) for a brighter future.

He was also given the visionary qualities to see this through his 11th house Pisces Moon conjunct Venus. Traditionaly, Venus in Pisces can be interpreted as a love of a monk. In the second Pisces decanate (Cancer) it becomes purely sacrificial without asking or expecting personal reward. This is one of the chart factors that automatically indicates an elevation of the Taurus-Scorpio polarity to higher levels. Otherwise there would be too much self-greed in the Taurus Ascendent and Node for Reverend King's mission to be accomplished. As such, the Pisces Moon and Venus along with the Sagittarius Saturn pull the life style off the physical plane, giving it more of a higher minded, ethereal quality.

The Saturn-Moon-Mars T square shows this to be a chart of enormous power, with most of it manifesting through the 8th house Saturn in Sagittarius (Leo decanate), symbolic of a martyr-like hero's death which comes to inspire regenerative life in the hearts of others. This Saturn is also one of the points of his Jupiter-Neptune-Saturn Grand Trine, indicating how much

his life as well as his death would be influenced by
external circumstances.

In his 5th house of creativity, we find Neptune in
Virgo forming an out of sign trine to his Sagittarius
Saturn. First, the Saturn-Neptune trine indicates that
this was to be a very important incarnation for him;
and second, the Virgo Neptune was to aid him in creating the dream of an ideal. He was to leave an impression that if man could believe something (Neptune), he
could work (Saturn) to make it come true.

Jupiter in the 12th house is always found in the
charts of those souls who have already received the
the inner teachings on the higher levels. They come
into this life with a deep inner sense of wisdom and
fairness.

Pluto in the 3rd house indicates the ability to be a
dynamic communicator, reaching people on the subconscious level where raw emotion (Cancer) is in its
pure state. In order for the full mission to be accomplished, the rest of the chart would have to show scope
of vision, perspective and balance. The Mars-Saturn
opposition speaks about the ancient teachings of the
past (Saturn in Sagittarius the sign of philosophy in
the house of legacy) as well as what should be done
about the future (Mars in Gemini conjunct the Ascendant of the chart of the United States).

This Saturn-Mars opposition also speaks about
achieving a balance between the impatience of youth
(Mars) and the wisdom of maturity (Saturn). The
placement falls in the 2nd and 8th houses, personal
values opposed to other people's values. Mars tradi-
tionally becomes a crusader when posited in Gemini
or Aquarius, and here we find the Aquarian Mercury
in mutual reception with the Gemini Mars. In addition,
they are in trine, giving Reverend King a clear channel
to express his message for the future (Mercury in
Aquarius in the 10th house) through verbal actions
(Mars in Gemini in the 2nd house of values.)

His 12th house Uranus in Aries was to bring out an

awareness of a new beginning, and with his Capricorn Sun he would dedicate his whole life to that purpose. Since the moon rules memory, and his Mercury (the planet through which the message came) forms a conjunction with America's Moon in Aquarius, we can rest assured that even if at times it may not appear so, his message will unquestionably be well-remembered.

Going back to the soul level and his Taurus North Node in the first house, this incarnation was for him to build in thought the principles of creative love and harmony. Surely, this was a forgotten message from the past (Capricorn) that had to be reinforced in human consciousness at the time of his incarnation.

PARAMAHANSA YOGANANDA

Here we have an example of how the chart with the Nodes can bring about the energy for a higher form of earth life.

The Taurus North Node is always an indication of a builder. While many choose to apply it physically, Yogananda attuned himself to the finer Taurean rays of creative love. As a mystic (Uranus conjunct South Node in Scorpio) and spiritual teacher (Neptune in Gemini) he has reached the hearts of aspirants all over the globe.

It is interesting to note that his way of life as a Yogi, which is so opposite to the American way of life, also shows up in the chart. His Capricorn Sun is in direct opposition to America's Sun, while his Leo Moon is also in opposition to America's Moon. Yet both Yogananda and the Untied States have the same Libra Saturn, which denotes a karmic mission to establish tranquillity.

The Guru's purpose was to come to America and plant new seeds (Mars in Aries) of spiritual desire (Jupiter in Aries) in a land already too filled with personal selfishness.

In reading the chart of a great mystic we must have

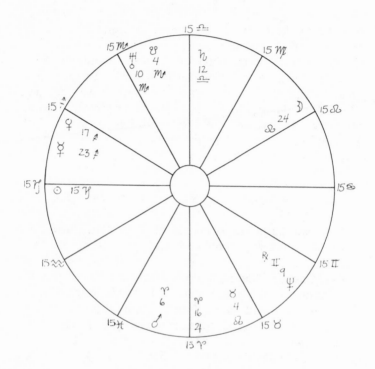

PARAMAHANSA YOGANANDA

1—5—1893

GORAKHPUR, INDIA

a different understanding of the Nodes, for such a soul would have already transcended any negative karma from previous incarnations. Thus, the South Node becomes the avenue or channel through which all the knowledge and wisdom of the universe learned in past lives can be brought into use during the current incarnation.

Yogananda had reached the level of consciousness where he could see his current life as one pearl on a string of pearls in the circle of Eternal Life. As such we see the Scorpio South Node not as residue to be eliminated, but rather as the symbol of past incarnation building blocks upon which the present-life Taurus North Node was now to be laid as a cornerstone.

Through the Uranus-South Node conjunction in Scorpio, Yogananda entered this incarnation after having already acquired the mystical secrets of insight at the very highest transmuted levels of Scorpionic awareness.

Through the Taurus North Node, he presented his wisdom with elementary simplicity, as had always been the pattern of great teachers before him. His own study followed through a line of tradition (Capricorn Sun) and yet he introduced a new concept of God to the Western world.

His Jupiter-Moon-Mercury Grand Trine throws particular emphasis on his Leo Moon. Mercury is in the Leo decanate of Sagittarius, while Jupiter is in the Leo decanate of Aries. The Moon itself, which represents Mother, is posited in the sign of Father. Living this incarnation in a male body, Yogananda was guided to realize how important it would be for all males of the world to be able to see God as the Divine Mother. He knew that this would enable man to develop the highest sensitivity to the feminine principle that creative love and gentle understanding conquers all things!

His own love was so great (Venus in Sagittarius, Venus-ruled North Node) that it was impossible to hold it inside. In 32 years he personally gave his teachings to over 100,000 people.

The physical plane materialism so common to the Taurus North Node manifested itself through the ashrams, healing centers, and retreats that Yogananda established. He was guided to do this so that long after his physical life was over, the world could still feel the impact of his message.

This horoscope is a fine example of how the pure science of astrology is still in its infancy. If one were to attempt interpretation according to currently-accepted standards the reading might be as follows:

Venus in Sagittarius opposed by Neptune in Gemini shows inconstancy in love, plus much lower mind confusion. Mercury in its fall in Sagittarius trine Jupiter in Aries indicates tendencies to jump to conclusions, and scatter oneself into unconnected areas.

The Leo Moon shows too much ego stemming from an overbearing mother. In addition it is one of the indicators of excessive alcoholism, Mars conjunct Jupiter in Aries denotes selfishness, while the Capricorn Sun turns the whole chart NEGATIVE.

While each one of these statements has been shown to be empirically true for great numbers of people, not a single one is accurate here!

There are souls who have evolved to a higher astrology, and Yogananda was one of them. Having complete mastery over the Emotional Plane, no astrological statement based on personality would be applicable. When the great mystic left his physical body for the last time, observers noted that for more than 20 days there was not the slightest indication of bodily decay. Yogananda had also mastered the Physical Plane!

There is no limit to the levels of regeneration that the Scorpio South Node could have achieved in past incarnations. In addition, the Taurus North Node symbolizes the Eye of Illumination in the body of God.

MAHATMA GANDHI

Here we see the powerful impact of the Leo North Node. Its 10th house placement within 3 degrees of the Midheaven accounted for Gandhi's enormous strength in overcoming obstacles which eventually earned for him the reputation of being a veritable giant among men.

Leo symbolizes the conquerer, and in his life of service (Libra Sun in the 12th, Neptune in the 6th) Gandhi was able to transform the minds of over 20 million men, women and children without raising a finger.

The Jupiter-Pluto conjunction in his 7th house spelled out the monumental task he was to perform for others. To do this, he first had to commit himself to the complete sacrifice of personal desire (Neptune in Aries in the 6th).

At the time of his birth, India had been thoroughly divided due to age-old British rule. Literally thousands of sects and conflicting groups were preventing the country from reaching unification. Bloodshed in the streets was a common occurrence as each faction battled for its own supremacy. The 4th house indicates the ways in which one sees one's homeland, and with Gandhi's South Node there, he would have seen how the Aquarian individualism, with all its accompanying rebelliousness to any order, was indeed killing the country he loved so dearly.

In a land that had already witnessed so much violence, what good could be achieved by one more aggressive approach? Through his Libra Sun, Gandhi chose the opposite path.

Early in life he had become a successful and prosperous lawyer (Saturn in Sagittarius in the 2nd), but ultimately he could not ignore the far greater mission that was to be his destiny. With this same Sagittarius Saturn in the Aries decanate of the sign, he was to strive for liberation through unification. Always dedicated to the principles of his Leo North Node, he strove to bring

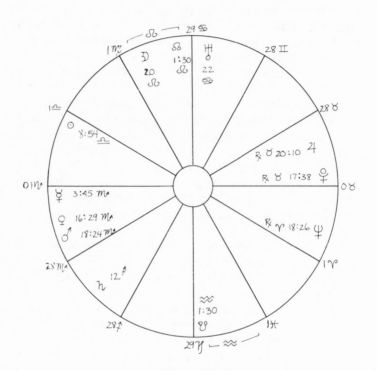

MAHATMA GANDHI

10—2—1869

PORBANDAR, INDIA

all the inharmonious factions (Libra Sun afflicted) together.

We often find some evidence of martyrdom inherent in the sign Leo, and with his Moon, North Node and Midheaven there, Gandhi was perfectly willing to attempt India's unification single-handedly, using himself as an example to others.

He worked long and hard on destroying all the lower parts of his own being, with the full understanding that before one can transform a nation, one must conquer himself. Through the three Scorpio planets in the 1st house, he nearly brought about his own death while trying to transform the stubbornness of others (Jupiter-Pluto in the 7th opposing Venus-Mars in the 1st).

Eventually Gandhi's hunger strikes (Uranus in Cancer square Neptune in the 6th) became world famous. His method of passive resistance (Aquarius South Node, Libra Sun in the 12th) was no longer folly but would indeed liberate the entire country as well as be adopted as a primary future method of political expression throughout the world.

Gandhi's South Node in Aquarius indicates prior lifetimes in which he developed the concepts of humane understanding. Along with his Libra Sun in the 12th which brings much of his past karma forward, this would make him totally opposed to all forms of violence in the present incarnation.

From a prosperous profession in his youth, Gandhi left the world with only three possessions—his rice bowl, his loin cloth and his eyeglasses! Had it not been for his enormous humility, he would never have been able to achieve his Leo mission. Certainly, his life is a picture of one who stooped to conquer!

ALLEGORY

. . . And it was morning as God stood before his twelve children and into each of them planted the seed of human life. One by one each child stepped forward to receive his appointed gift.

"To you Aries I give my seed first that you might have the honor of planting it. That for every seed you plant one million more will multiply in your hand. You will not have time to see the seed grow for everything you plant creates more that must be planted. You will be the first to penetrate the soil of men's minds with My Idea. But it is not your job to nourish the Idea nor to question it. Your life is action and the only action I ascribe to you is to begin making men aware of My Creation. For your good work I give you the virtue of Self Esteem."

Quietly Aries stepped back to his place.

"To you Taurus I give the power to build the seed into substance. Your job is a great one requiring patience for you must finish all that has been started or the seeds will be wasted to the wind. You are not to question nor change your mind in the middle nor to depend on others for what I ask you to do. For this I give you the gift of Strength. Use it wisely."

And Taurus stepped back into place.

"To you Gemini I give the questions without answers so that you may bring to all an understanding of what man sees around him. You will never know why men speak or listen, but in your quest for the answer you will find my gift of Knowledge."

And Gemini stepped back into place.

"To you Cancer I ascribe the task of teaching men about emotion. My Idea is for you to cause them laughter and tears so that all they see and think develops fullness from inside. For this I give you the gift of Family, that your fullness may multiply."

And Cancer stepped back to his place.

"To you Leo I give the job of displaying My Creation in all its brilliance to the world. But you must be careful of pride and always remember that it is My Creation, not yours. For if you forget this men will scorn you. There is much joy in the job I give to you if you but do it well. For this you are to have the gift of Honor."

And Leo stepped back to his place.

"To you Virgo I ask for an examination of all man has done with My Creation. You are to scrutinize his ways sharply and remind him of his errors so that through you My Creation may be perfected. For doing this I give you the gift of Purity of Thought."

And Virgo stepped back to his place.

"To you Libra I give the mission of service, that man may be mindful of his duties to others. That he may learn cooperation as well as the ability to reflect the other side of his actions. I will put you everywhere there is discord, and for your efforts I will give you the gift of Love."

And Libra stepped back in place.

"To you Scorpio I give a very difficult task. You will have the ability to know the minds of men, but I do not permit you to speak about what you learn. Many times you will be pained by what you see, and in your pain you will turn away from Me and forget that it is not I but the perversion of My Idea that is causing your pain. You will see so much of man that you will come to know him as animal and wrestle so much with his animal instincts in yourself that you will lose your way; but when you finally come back to Me, Scorpio, I have for you the supreme gift of Purpose."

And Scorpio stepped back.

"Sagittarius, I ask you to make men laugh for amidst their misunderstanding of My Idea they become bitter. Through laughter you are to give man hope, and through hope turn his eyes back to Me. You will touch many lives if but only for a moment, and you will know the restlessness in every life you touch. To you Sagittarius I give the gift of Infinite Abundance, that you may spread wide enough to reach into every corner of darkness and bring it light."

And Sagittarius stepped back into place.

"Of you Capricorn I ask the toil of your brow, that you might teach men to work. Your task is not an easy one for you will feel all of man's labors on your shoulders; but for the yoke of your burdens I put the responsibility of man in your hands."

And Capricorn stepped back into place.

"To you Aquarius I give the concept of future that man might see other possibilities. You will have the pain of loneliness for I do not allow you to personalize My Love. But for turning man's eyes to new possibilities I give you the gift of Freedom, that in your liberty you may continue to serve mankind whenever he needs you."

And Aquarius stepped back into place.

"To you Pisces I give the most difficult task of all. I ask you to collect all of man's sorrow and return it to me. Your tears are to be ultimately My tears. The sorrow you will absorb is the effect of man's misunderstanding My Idea, but you are to give him compassion that he may try again. For this the most difficult task of all I give the greatest gift of all. You will be the only one of My twelve children to understand Me. But this gift of understanding is for you, Pisces for when you try to spread it to man he will not listen."

And Pisces stepped back into place.

. . . Then God said "You each have a part of My Idea. You must not mistake that part for all of My Idea, nor may you desire to trade parts with each other. For each of you is perfect, but you will not know that until all twelve of you are ONE. For then the whole of My Idea will be revealed to each of you."

And the children left, each determined to do his job best that he might receive his gift. But none fully understood his task or his gift, and when they returned puzzled God said, "You each believe that other gifts are better. Therefore I will allow you to trade." And for the moment each child was elated as he considered all the possibilities of his new mission.

But God smiled as he said "You will return to Me

many times asking to be relieved of your mission, and each time I will grant you your wish. You will go through countless incarnations before you complete the original mission I have prescribed for you. I give you countless time in which to do it, but only when it is done can you be with Me."

CONCLUSION

The experiences of life shade each other much like the interplay of colors in a finely-woven tapestry. Each thought in the foreground has come from the background and will return to the background again. The overlays of dreams, ideas and actions seem endless, sometimes perhaps, even senseless. Yet, each is part of the fiber from which the thread of life is spun.

When man can see and understand his ideas, as well as the circumstances that occur in his life as part of the thread he alone is spinning, he will start to develop the substance from within that makes him real from without.

The Moon's Nodes help man to understand the nature of his purpose, the reason he has been deemed worthy of life. Instead of seeing life as a collection of unrelated coincidences, man can stand a little taller with the knowledge that all he ever aspires to be, he already was—and more. All he has to do is find himself.

APPENDIX

THE MOON'S NORTH NODE POSITIONS

1850-1899

Jan. 1, 1850—May 10, 1851	Leo
May 11, 1851—Nov. 25, 1852	Cancer
Nov. 26, 1852—June 16, 1854	Gemini
June 17, 1854—Jan. 3, 1856	Taurus
Jan. 4, 1856—July 23, 1857	Aries
July 24, 1857—Feb. 9, 1859	Pisces
Feb. 10, 1859—Aug. 29, 1860	Aquarius
Aug. 30, 1860—Mar. 18, 1862	Capricorn
Mar. 19, 1862—Oct. 6, 1863	Sagittarius
Oct. 7, 1863—April 25, 1865	Scorpio
April 26, 1865—Nov. 12, 1866	Libra
Nov. 13, 1866—June 1, 1868	Virgo
June 2, 1868—Dec. 20, 1869	Leo
Dec. 21, 1869—July 9, 1871	Cancer
July 10, 1871—Jan. 25, 1873	Gemini
Jan. 26, 1873—Aug. 15, 1874	Taurus
Aug. 16, 1874—Mar. 3, 1876	Aries
Mar. 4, 1876—Sept. 21, 1877	Pisces
Sept. 22, 1877—April 10, 1879	Aquarius
April 11, 1879—Oct. 28, 1880	Capricorn
Oct. 29, 1880—May 17, 1882	Sagittarius
May 18, 1882—Dec. 5, 1883	Scorpio
Dec. 6, 1883—June 24, 1885	Libra
June 25, 1885—Jan. 12, 1887	Virgo
Jan. 13, 1887—July 31, 1888	Leo
Aug. 1, 1888—Feb. 17, 1890	Cancer

Feb. 18, 1890—Sept. 7, 1891	Gemini
Sept. 8, 1891—Mar. 26, 1893	Taurus
Mar. 27, 1893—Oct. 13, 1894	Aries
Oct. 14, 1894—May 2, 1896	Pisces
May 3, 1896—Nov. 20, 1897	Aquarius
Nov. 21, 1897—June 9, 1899	Capricorn
June 10, 1899—Dec. 31, 1899	Sagittarius

1900-1949

Jan. 1, 1900—Dec. 28, 1900	Sagittarius
Dec. 29, 1900—July 17, 1902	Scorpio
July 18, 1902—Feb. 4, 1904	Libra
Feb. 5, 1904—Aug. 23, 1905	Virgo
Aug. 24, 1905—Mar. 13, 1907	Leo
Mar. 14, 1907—Sept. 29, 1908	Cancer
Sept. 30, 1908—April 18, 1910	Gemini
April 19, 1910—Nov. 7, 1911	Taurus
Nov. 8, 1911—May 26, 1913	Aries
May 27, 1913—Dec. 13, 1914	Pisces
Dec. 14, 1914—July 2, 1916	Aquarius
July 3, 1916—Jan. 19, 1918	Capricorn
Jan. 20, 1918—Aug. 9, 1919	Sagittarius
Aug. 10, 1919—Feb. 26, 1921	Scorpio
Feb. 27, 1921—Sept. 15, 1922	Libra
Sept. 16, 1922—April 4, 1924	Virgo
April 5, 1924—Oct. 22, 1925	Leo
Oct. 23, 1925—May 12, 1927	Cancer
May 13, 1927—Nov. 28, 1928	Gemini
Nov. 29, 1928—June 18, 1930	Taurus
June 19, 1930—Jan. 6, 1932	Aries
Jan. 7, 1932—July 25, 1933	Pisces
July 26, 1933—Feb. 12, 1935	Aquarius
Feb. 13, 1935—Sept. 1, 1936	Capricorn
Sept. 2, 1936—Mar. 21, 1938	Sagittarius
Mar. 22, 1938—Oct. 9, 1939	Scorpio
Oct. 10, 1939—April 27, 1941	Libra
April 28, 1941—Nov. 15, 1942	Virgo
Nov. 16, 1942—June, 3, 1944	Leo
June 4, 1944—Dec. 23, 1945	Cancer

Dec. 24, 1945—July 11, 1947	Gemini
July 12, 1947—Jan. 28, 1949	Taurus
Jan. 29, 1949—Dec. 31, 1949	Aries

1950-1999

Jan. 1, 1950—Aug. 17, 1950	Aries
Aug. 18, 1950—Mar. 7, 1952	Pisces
Mar. 8, 1952—Oct. 2, 1953	Aquarius
Oct. 3, 1953—April 12, 1955	Capricorn
April 13, 1955—Nov. 4, 1956	Sagittarius
Nov. 5, 1956—May 21, 1958	Scorpio
May 22, 1958—Dec. 8, 1959	Libra
Dec. 9, 1959—July 3, 1961	Virgo
July 4, 1961—Jan. 13, 1963	Leo
Jan. 14, 1963—Aug. 5, 1964	Cancer
Aug. 6, 1964—Feb. 21, 1966	Gemini
Feb. 22, 1966—Sept. 10, 1967	Taurus
Sept. 11, 1967—April 3, 1969	Aries
April 4, 1969—Oct. 15, 1970	Pisces
Oct. 16, 1970—May 5, 1972	Aquarius
May 6, 1972—Nov. 22, 1973	Capricorn
Nov. 23, 1973—June 12, 1975	Sagittarius
June 13, 1975—Dec. 29, 1976	Scorpio
Dec. 30, 1976—July 19, 1978	Libra
July 20, 1978—Feb. 5, 1980	Virgo
Feb. 6, 1980—Aug. 25, 1981	Leo
Aug. 26, 1981—Mar. 14, 1983	Cancer
Mar. 15, 1983—Oct.1, 1984	Gemini
Oct. 2, 1984—April 20, 1986	Taurus
April 21, 1986—Nov. 8, 1987	Aries
Nov. 9, 1987—May 28, 1989	Pisces
May 29, 1989—Dec. 15, 1990	Aquarius
Dec. 16, 1990—July 4, 1992	Capricorn
July 5, 1992—Jan. 21, 1994	Sagittarius
Jan. 22, 1994—Aug. 11, 1995	Scorpio
Aug. 12, 1995—Feb. 27, 1997	Libra
Feb. 28, 1997—Sept. 17, 1998	Virgo
Sept. 18, 1998—Dec. 31, 1999	Leo